Learning from the Stranger

Learning from the **Stranger**

CHRISTIAN FAITH
AND CULTURAL DIVERSITY

DAVID I. SMITH

WILLIAM B. EERDMANS PUBLISHING COMPANY
GRAND RAPIDS, MICHIGAN / CAMBRIDGE, U.K.

Published 2009 by

Wm. B. Eerdmans Publishing Co.

2140 Oak Industrial Drive N.E., Grand Rapids, Michigan 49505 /

P.O. Box 163, Cambridge CB3 9PU U.K.

Printed in the United States of America

14 13 12 11 10 09   7 6 5 4 3 2 1

Library of Congress Cataloging-in-Publication Data

Smith, David, 1966-

Learning from the stranger: Christian faith and cultural diversity /
David I. Smith.

p.   cm.

Includes bibliographical references (p.   ) and index.

ISBN 978-0-8028-2463-9 (pbk.: alk. paper)

1. Multiculturalism — Religious aspects — Christianity.

2. Christianity and culture.   I. Title.

BR115.C8S5838   2009

261 — dc22

2008046906

www.eerdmans.com

Contents

120234

Acknowledgments

As with any substantial piece of writing, this book arises from many interactions and forms of support, not all of which I am likely to succeed in mentioning. My colleagues in the Department of Germanic and Asian Languages and on the Cross-Cultural Engagement Committee at Calvin College provided the necessary collegial context in which to think, and an invitation to lecture to freshmen on intercultural learning as part of Prelude, Calvin's orientation program, provided the occasion to develop first drafts of Chapter 2. Early discussions with Irene Konyndyk, Lissa Schwander, and Claudia Beversluis helped give initial shape to the book, as did an invitation from Karen Exoo and Lance Engbers that led to fruitful conversations. An interim course release in 2007 provided space to develop Chapter 3, for which my thanks go to Dean Ward and Calvin College. An invitation from Ed Klotz to lead two weeklong workshops on internationalizing the curriculum at John Brown University, as well as discussions with the participants, also helped in thinking through these chapters. Participation in a summer seminar on biblical theology for the disciplines led by James K. A. Smith and Richard Middleton in the summer of 2007 provided the ideal context for working on Chapter 4 — I offer my thanks to them, to the Lilly Fellows Program in Humanities and the Arts at Valparaiso University for supporting the workshop, and to my fellow participants for stimulating discussion and fellowship.

Various friends and colleagues read parts of the manuscript and offered helpful feedback — my thanks to Kate Avila, Brad Baurain, Barbara Carvill, Yvonne Ferwerda, Daniel McWhirter, Jacqueline Rhodes,

James K. A. Smith, and Lynda Warner. Barbara Carvill in particular has long taught me how to think about these matters. My thanks also to Jon Pott at Eerdmans for being supportive from the start. It has been a blessing to have a family who have not only tolerated but have been interested in and helped with the project — thank you Julia, Nathaniel, Miriam, and Amy. The failings, of course, remain my own — both the failings in the book and the failings in this list of assistance received.

Several sections of the book are adapted from articles first published in the *Journal of Christianity and Foreign Languages:* parts of Chapter 5 are from "Tourists, Guests, and Why we Learn Other Languages," *Journal of Christianity and Foreign Languages* 4 (2003): 3-9. Parts of Chapter 7 are adapted from "Pentecost, Perplexity and Language Learning," *Journal of Christianity and Foreign Languages* 5 (2004): 3-9; and "Cross-Cultural Learning and Christian History," *Journal of Christianity and Foreign Languages* 6 (2005): 3-7. Parts of Chapter 6 draw upon earlier work with Barbara Carvill in our book *The Gift of the Stranger: Faith, Hospitality, and Foreign Language Learning* (Grand Rapids: Eerdmans, 2000). Chapter 1 is a revised version of an article published in *Perspectives:* "How Not to Bless the Nations," *Perspectives* (December 2005): 6-11.

I am grateful to Pearson Education, Inc., for permission to reproduce an extract from Ralph Linton's *The Study of Man* in Chapter 2; and to St. Vladimir's Seminary Press for permission to reproduce a hymn by Ephrem the Syrian in Chapter 7. All Scripture quotations, unless otherwise indicated, come from *The Holy Bible: Today's New International Version* (TNIV), copyright 2002 and 2004 by International Bible Society and used by permission of Zondervan.

RELINQUISHING THE CENTER

I had been at the school for a couple of days, watching classes, reading policy documents, interviewing parents and students. My task was to review the Spanish programs at a private Christian school, and to offer feedback and recommendations to the school administration. Both teachers and administrators were committed to high-quality education, and this review process had been initiated by the school with the aim of evaluating, and where necessary improving, its own programs. As I observed, interviewed, and discussed, I found teachers, parents, and administrators who believed in and were committed to the school's mission, and were having a positive impact on the lives of the predominantly white, English-speaking students.[1]

I spent part of one morning interviewing middle school students. Why, I asked them, are you learning a second language? They had all learned to articulate a specific Christian rationale for their studies: to share God's love with speakers of Spanish, they told me, was the goal of their language classes. Do you think, I continued, you'll use your Spanish after you leave school? One or two thought they might, but most responded with a resounding negative. A little surprised, I asked why they thought that their Spanish would never be put to use. "Because I am not going to be a missionary," was the immediate and general response. I knew that at least two of the large local churches had missionary connections with Latin America, and that the school also involved students in mission trips to the region. "Sharing God's love" apparently also translated rather easily as Christian-speak for "engaging in missionary work" in the minds of students.

1

Learning Spanish seemed to be firmly associated in the minds of many students with the needs of the career missionary, yielding a straightforward syllogism: Spanish is for missions; I am not called to be a missionary; therefore I will have no use for Spanish. I pursued the matter further, asking how many speakers of Spanish they thought were living in the United States. "Oh, lots," they replied. "On the West Coast, and in the L.A. airport." Hispanic folk were, apparently, believed to be abundant but distant. When it came to many of these students' understanding of their place in a world of over 6,000 languages and even more cultures, there was clear room for growth.

A few hours after this conversation I talked with a parent, a local doctor, who was still visibly angry regarding an incident that had occurred earlier that day at the medical center where she worked. A Hispanic woman with limited English-speaking skills had been unable to obtain prompt medical care for her baby because the reception staff at the medical center spoke no Spanish. The doctor, who did speak Spanish, had been gone for lunch. The lady and her baby had been shuttled off to a hospital some distance away, in the hope that the staff there would know how to deal with her. After hearing this story, I went online and checked the most recent U.S. census statistics. There were around 100,000 Hispanics living within an hour's drive of the school (which was not located within a thousand miles of the Los Angeles airport!). The sense of disconnect was stark.

Before my visit, some tenth-grade students had completed some questionnaires. One of the questions, in an attempt to assess whether students had internalized the Spanish department's articulation of its mission, asked whether Spanish classes had helped each student "to break down barriers of language and culture in order to communicate God's love to people around you." There were many variants on the comment that learning Spanish made it possible to tell more people about Jesus. Individual students wrote of how knowing some Spanish had been a great help when on a mission trip, because they could "tell Spanish [sic] people about God." Sometimes the assumption appeared to be that the Christian gospel — or even the experience of God's love — basically resides among English speakers; there were comments to the effect that we would not be able to spread God's love very far with English only, since so much of the world's population is not English-speaking. In many of the responses, it seemed that the term "sharing" in the phrase "sharing God's love" was understood as more parallel to a phrase such as "I'll share my candy with you" than to "Let's share an apartment next year."

The picture of the world that underlies such thoughts and comments is increasingly out-of-date. A hundred years ago (although not in all preceding centuries) it was plausible to think of the Western world as the Christian center from which missionary activity radiated out. Recent decades have, however, seen rapid demographic shifts. Philip Jenkins vividly sketches the basic ways in which the picture is changing:

> Between 1900 and 2000, the number of Christians in Africa grew from 10 million to over 360 million. . . . Already today, Africans and Asians represent some 30 percent of all Christians. . . . [By 2050] there should be around three billion Christians in the world, of whom only around one fifth or fewer will be non-Hispanic whites.[2]

Eminent missiologist Andrew Walls comments that "the most striking feature of Christianity at the beginning of the third millennium is that it is predominantly a non-Western religion."[3] Back when it all began, when Jesus said, "Go into all the world," he was not standing in London or Washington, D.C.; now, at the start of the twenty-first century after Christ, the Holy Spirit continues to blow where he wills, and to leave our comfortable assumptions scattered in his wake.

In addition to the assumption that Christian language learning is for mission trips to take the gospel from English-speaking to non-English-speaking cultures, the questionnaire responses exhibited another troubling tendency. Students commented that language learning was useful when traveling overseas because "now they can understand me better," or because "they eventually got my main points," or because the locals showed their visitors more respect because of the students' ability to speak some Spanish. In comment after comment, the implied underlying relationship with native speakers of Spanish was one in which the fruit of language learning was a situation in which *they* learn to understand and respect *me*. Learning their language might be useful insofar as it can help me achieve this. With one or two (but only one or two) notable exceptions, the thirty or so students made no mention in their responses of listening to and learning *from*

Spanish speakers, or of what Spanish speakers might have to *teach* them about the love of God, or of Spanish speakers as more than needy recipients of the students' earnest communications.

These were, of course, brief responses to a questionnaire given out by a teacher and appended to a test, so too much weight should not be placed on them — I hope and trust that many of the students exhibited more mature and complex attitudes when actually interacting with Hispanics than they managed to articulate on the survey sheet. However, the strength of the overall trends was striking. When I met with teachers and administrators — who were quite clear that these student perceptions did not properly reflect their aims as Christian educators — we began to discuss strategies for challenging these trends. Were, for instance, insights from Hispanic theologians and Christian leaders used in chapel services and classroom devotions? Were Hispanics invited to speak in the school, not only about "exotic" features of Hispanic cultures, but on topics of shared importance in the school community? How could respect for what Hispanics have to say be modeled in front of students? Did the language curriculum deal adequately with culture alongside its focus on communication skills? Were the images of Hispanics encountered in language learning materials stereotypical? In brief, how could the school's ongoing practices reflect genuine hospitality to the stranger?

What I have just described are the responses of a small number of young students whose understanding of the world was still in the process of formation. However, their comments do seem to fit with wider patterns in both secular and Christian culture. In the mainstream of English-speaking American culture, the supremacy and adequacy of English is commonly taken for granted, and learning from other cultures and languages is not a high cultural priority. Within Christian settings, most books concerned with intercultural learning are marketed to those interested in missions, and appear to assume that the learning will be applied primarily in missionary settings. Many such texts do embrace an "incarnational" approach that stresses the value of humility and service;[4] nevertheless, the use in educational settings of a missionary frame as the prime justification for learning other languages and cultures too easily slips into a number of unhelpful but widespread tendencies. These include the temptation to view such learning as irrelevant if one does not feel called to overseas missionary work (or per-

haps to overtly multicultural church ministry), the temptation to prior-
itize our ability to contribute to other cultures over their ability to
speak to us, the temptation to always elevate our perceived competence over their perceived need, and the increasingly dated notion that
Christian witness involves the one-way export of truth from a largely
English-speaking Western church to a rather vaguely perceived but
supposedly largely heathen rest of the world. These perceptions
amount, of course, to a remarkably poor theology of mission, one that
would be squarely rejected by contemporary missiologists and
thoughtful missionaries. They remain, however, all too common, and
suggest the need to question common assumptions. Pointing this out
is not a vote against missions, merely an indication that even the apparently unselfish desire to share the gospel gets infiltrated by our own
cultural egocentricity, so reluctant are we to relinquish pictures of the
world that place ourselves at the center.

This book is about why it is important for Christians (perhaps especially, though not exclusively, Western Christians), whatever their
particular calling in life might be, to better engage in learning to deal
with cultural and linguistic difference. It explores how cultural difference raises issues that need facing, the kinds of learning that are
needed in order to face them, how these kinds of learning connect with
Christian growth, and the theological reasons why we should take all
this very seriously. It is almost time to let the rest of the book speak for
itself, but a few comments are in order about my specific intentions.

First, a few words about what is meant by "culture." Linguistic
differences are relatively obvious, at least at the everyday level — we
generally know when we are not understanding someone else's words.
Cultural differences can be a little subtler, and many different defini-
tions of culture have been offered over the years and across the disciplines. We use the word "culture" in various ways. Sometimes it refers
to a particular set of refined accomplishments ("He just has no culture!") or works of inspiration ("the achievements of French culture")
in a way that implies that only some people are "cultured" or have
"culture." That is not its meaning here. In these pages, the term is used
more in its basic anthropological sense, to refer to the patterns of being, doing, and thinking that human communities share and to which
they assign meanings, as opposed to the natural processes of the non-
human creation.

Consider, for example, the difference between a tree branch waving in the wind and a human hand waving. The tree branch's movement shows the effect of natural causes rather than the tree's intention to say something, and the same kind of branch would wave in the same way in the same kind of wind the world over. The human hand is probably sending a message, engaging in a behavior shaped by human intentions that calls upon others to interpret it in particular ways. As such, it varies between human communities. North Americans tend to wave good-bye with the hand up, the palm out, and the hand making side-to-side motions that also involve the forearm. Italians and Greeks often wave good-bye with the arm extended, the palm up, and the fingers curling back and forth, a gesture that most North Americans would interpret as beckoning someone to "come here" rather than as saying good-bye.[5] Unlike the jerk of your lower leg that follows if your knee is tapped in a certain way, these varieties of waving are not programmed reflex actions, but rather part of complex patterns of meaning woven among particular groups of people. This is a major part of how humans function. Human beings do not simply exist in the world, but build up particular, varying ways of acting and interacting, shaping artifacts, telling stories, building dwellings, inventing names, and so on. In this sense of the word, culture is not something achieved by a few. It is our way of being in the world together.

While it is often convenient to refer to national or geographical categories in order to locate particular cultural realities (I just did so when I mentioned Italians, Greeks, and North Americans), it should be borne in mind that this is only a loose shorthand. Cultural patterns do not start and stop cleanly at national borders, and the inhabitants of a given country are never all identical in their ways of thinking and behaving. Cultures are a feature of communities, but those communities may overlap, live in the same geographical space, and include some who do not play along with the norm. Some cultural generalizations can be made about societies (North Americans are generally dependent on cars), but there will always be exceptions (there are in North America Amish communities that choose not to use motorized transport). Many people live in and learn to navigate more than one cultural world — consider, for instance, an African American child who attends a predominantly white school and then works as a doctor in an area where refugee families have been resettled. Throughout the book, the examples discussed are assigned to particular cultural groups, but it should be kept in mind that members of any group are not identical and that cultural realities are constantly interacting and shifting.

When talking about learning amid cultural difference my preferred term will be "intercultural" learning. The two most common related terms are "multicultural" and "cross-cultural." The former certainly points to some of the same issues, but it often specifically evokes the politics of race. Cultural differences and racial justice are certainly connected, but the latter is not the primary focus of this book. "Cross-cultural" is closer to the mark, but I have in most places preferred to refer to "intercultural" learning as perhaps more strongly suggesting a learning process than affects both parties, not just a crossing of boundaries but a way of interacting in which both sides can learn.

The book is not a textbook on all aspects of intercultural learning, and it will not substitute for more detailed study of particular cultures. It is not a book about social policy, and does not propose ways of handling immigration or foreign policy. Its primary aim is to set a trajectory for future learning, to make sense in Christian terms of the challenges and joys of learning cultures and languages and learning from strangers. In the chapters that follow, I do not assume that readers are planning to be missionaries, at least in the common sense of the word — or necessarily that they are planning not to be. I also do not assume that readers have any foreseeable plans to live or serve overseas — though those that do might also find the book helpful. I am centrally concerned with what it might mean to live well where we are simply *as Christians* in the world as we find it at the present historical moment. For this reason I do assume an inclination on the part of readers to value the Christian life, although those who do not share this inclination are of course welcome to listen in.

While writing I have mainly had Christian students (and those who educate them) in mind, though of course I nurture the hope that readers whose learning is not currently taking place within an educational institution will also find the book helpful. I am aware that readers will bring a range of cultural identities to the book. I have sought to write in a way that might serve diverse readers, but the book will inevitably still reflect my own particular identity. I am British[6] (but have lived in Germany, Canada, and the United States), white, a college professor, and an active member of a Reformed Christian denomination. If any of this makes me a stranger to you, I hope that you will be able to bear with me and find things to learn in the pages that follow.

There are basically three parts to the book. The first appears at intervals. Chapters 1, 4, and 7 together provide an overarching theological frame. I have chosen largely to avoid appeal to scattered individual verses of Scripture. Such an approach risks modeling poor interpretive practices and the tendency to find verses to fit any argument.[7] (If I were allowed to record all of your utterances for two weeks, and then choose any ten at random and sequence them in any order I liked, I wonder how many different things I could make you say?) Instead, I have chosen to set up guideposts in Chapters 1, 4, and 7 by engaging in close readings of particular biblical passages, and to sequence them so as to reflect at least to some degree the larger narrative shape of the Bible.

This does not, of course, make me immune to error (my understanding of these passages has continued to develop as I have worked on this book); it also involves no claim to comprehensiveness — there are other passages that could equally well be explored. I merely hope that it shows serious, attentive engagement with what Scripture has to say on the matters at hand, and a willingness to get down into the fabric of the biblical text rather then staying at the level of broad thematic assertions. My intent is to invite you into the ongoing project of letting our cultural imaginations (and the ways we imagine culture) be challenged by Scripture, and not merely shaped by the shared assumptions of our society. In Chapter 1 we will start with Abraham, the "father of all who believe" (Romans 4:11).[8] Chapter 4 considers Jesus' take on the ethics of cultural difference, and Chapter 7 explores Pentecost and the early church as signposts to the intended Christian future.

Between these three chapters come two pairs of chapters. Chapters 2 and 3 explore further what is meant by culture and how it affects our perceptions, actions, and identities. If we think of culture superficially as consisting of a few exotic external behaviors — wearing grass skirts or bowler hats, eating with chopsticks or following baseball — then the connection with basic questions of faith and faithfulness seems limited. Chapters 2 and 3 explore some of the consequences of realizing that our very sense of self and of how to think, perceive, and behave is deeply shaped by local cultural patterns. The basic questions in these two chapters are: What is culture? How does it work? How does it shape us? How should we respond?

Chapters 5 and 6 focus on intercultural learning. They look first at some ways of approaching other cultures that fall short in terms of intercultural learning, probing their strengths and weaknesses. They then explore the positive side of the coin, exploring the processes involved in learning to live well amid cultural diversity, asking at the same time what connection these processes have to the processes of spiritual growth. These chapters sketch some contours of the kinds of learning that are demanded of us if we hope to live a life characterized by love of God and neighbor in a culturally diverse world.

My aim throughout is to offer a picture of how we need to learn and grow that moves beyond images of Christian intercultural learning as focused only on the safely distant and exotic, on pity for the needy, or on mission trips of longer or shorter duration. Learning from the stranger, I will argue, is a necessary component of genuinely loving one's neighbor. That is a calling facing each of us, whatever our stations in life.

CHAPTER 1

HOW NOT TO BLESS THE NATIONS

GENESIS 20:1-18

Now Abraham moved on from there into the region of the Negev and lived between Kadesh and Shur. For a while he stayed in Gerar, and there Abraham said of his wife Sarah, "She is my sister." Then Abimelek king of Gerar sent for Sarah and took her. But God came to Abimelek in a dream one night and said to him, "You are as good as dead because of the woman you have taken; she is a married woman."

Now Abimelek had not gone near her, so he said, "Lord, will you destroy an innocent nation? Did he not say to me, 'She is my sister,' and didn't she also say, 'He is my brother'? I have done this with a clear conscience and clean hands." Then God said to him in the dream, "Yes, I know you did this with a clear conscience, and so I have kept you from sinning against me. That is why I did not let you touch her. Now return the man's wife, for he is a prophet, and he will pray for you and you will live. But if you do not return her, you may be sure that you and all who belong to you will die."

Early the next morning Abimelek summoned all his officials, and when he told them all that had happened, they were very much afraid. Then Abimelek called Abraham in and said, "What have you done to us? How have I wronged you that you have brought such great guilt upon me and my kingdom? You have done things to me that should never be done." And Abimelek asked Abraham, "What was your reason for doing this?" Abraham replied, "I said to myself, 'There is surely no fear of God in this place, and they will kill me because of my wife.'"

"Besides, she really is my sister, the daughter of my father though not of my mother; and she became my wife. And when God had me wander from my father's household, I said to her, 'This is how you can show your love to me: Everywhere we go, say of me, "He is my brother."'"

Then Abimelek brought sheep and cattle and male and female slaves and gave them to Abraham, and he returned Sarah his wife to him. And Abimelek said, "My land is before you; live wherever you like."

To Sarah he said, "I am giving your brother a thousand shekels of silver. This is to cover the offense against you before all who are with you; you are completely vindicated."

Then Abraham prayed to God, and God healed Abimelek, his wife and his female slaves so they could have children again, for the LORD had kept all the women in Abimelek's household from conceiving because of Abraham's wife Sarah.

THE KING

The king was understandably upset. In a single night, it had all unraveled. What had started out as a most gratifying series of developments had taken a turn that would unseat anyone's peace of mind; divine death-threats in the dark night hours were not the best recipe for a restful sleep, and watching fear seep through his court was not his favorite way to start the day. And all because of that foreigner.

Before last night there had been no hint of trouble. A wealthy nomad from out east had turned up in Gerar and pitched his tents. Word had it that he had brought his sister along, and King Abimelek saw a chance to forge a potentially useful alliance.[1] He made the necessary arrangements to have her officially added to his harem.

And then what had seemed like a sensible strategy turned scary. God appeared to him in an unforgettably vivid dream and told him bluntly that he would die. This wandering foreigner, apparently, was a prophet, the woman was his wife, and Abimelek, who had taken her for his own, was in trouble. Abimelek protested that he could not have known she was the prophet's wife, that Abraham himself had declared her to be his sister and raised no complaint when she was sent for, that

Sarah had confirmed the claim, and that although Sarah was now in his residence, he had not yet been near her. God's tone remained stern — it was I who kept you from sinning against her, he pointed out, and you are to return good to this foreigner even though he deceived you and is in your power. At least God lifted the death sentence, provided Sarah was returned and Abraham's intercession was sought.

Abimelek woke early in a cold sweat, and his fear spread to his officials when he told them about the dream. Now he was about to face Abraham, his mind churning with a bewildering mixture of dread and anger, awe and protest. From pleasurable anticipation to fear for his life and loss of control over his choices, from ruler of the land to the recipient of a foreigner's mercy, all in a single night. The king was understandably upset.

> "Lord, will you destroy an innocent nation? Did he not say to me, 'She is my sister,' and didn't she also say, 'He is my brother'? I have done this with a clear conscience and clean hands." Then God said to him in the dream, "Yes, I know you did this with a clear conscience, and so I have kept you from sinning against me. That is why I did not let you touch her. Now return the man's wife, for he is a prophet, and he will pray for you and you will live. But if you do not return her, you may be sure that you and all who belong to you will die."
>
> GENESIS 20:4-7

THE STRANGER

Abraham was anxious. He entered cautiously, unsure exactly what to expect or why he had been summoned so early. It did not take long for the king of Gerar to get to the point: "What have you done to us? How have I wronged you that you have brought such great guilt upon me and my kingdom? You have done things to me that decent people just don't do!" Why, Abimelek wanted to know, would he pretend that his wife was his sister? Why would he stand by and let her be taken to another man's bed? What possible reason could he have had for quietly ushering others into evil, for bringing God's anger down on their heads?

Abraham stood silently for a while before replying, suddenly exposed in a public place far from home, his murky motives laid bare in the court of a foreign king. Abimelek's anger alone he could perhaps have braved, but there was now more than Abimelek involved. By way of Abimelek's dream, the questions were coming from God himself, the God whom Abraham had been following all these years.[2] *Why, Abraham, when I called you to be a blessing to the nations, why did you do this?*

Abraham's mind darted back involuntarily to the time when he had turned his steps toward Gerar. He had just witnessed the destruction of Sodom, Gomorrah, and the other cities of the plain. He had asked God to spare them for the sake of fifty, twenty, even ten righteous people, and God, far from haggling, seemed to be thinking along the same lines. The burning ruins bore shocking testimony to the absence of even ten whom God could regard as righteous. The anxiety that he already carried with him as one who wandered through other people's lands, dependent on their good will, was roused afresh: nothing in this part of the world but wickedness, people who might stoop to anything, especially concerning a man with wealth and a wife. Now his fear, a fear that had sustained repeated deception in the name of self-preservation wherever he had traveled, was laid bare before the gaze of a foreign king and his court.

> Early the next morning Abraham got up and returned to the place where he had stood before the LORD. He looked down toward Sodom and Gomorrah, toward all the land of the plain, and he saw dense smoke rising from the land, like smoke from a furnace.
>
> GENESIS 19:27-28

"I was afraid," he admitted. "I said to myself, 'There is surely no fear of God in this place, and they will kill me because of my wife.' Besides, she really is my sister, the daughter of my father though not of my mother; and she became my wife. And when God caused me to wander from my father's household, I said to her, 'This is how you can show your love to me: Everywhere we go, say of me, "He is my brother."'" Everywhere he had traveled, Abraham had been anxious.

IRONY

This story is found in Genesis 20, sandwiched between the promise to Abraham that Sarah would finally give birth to a son, a sign of God's covenant with the man who was to bless the nations, and the actual birth of Isaac. It is a story filled with irony. Abraham, the prophet, mumbles apologies while the Word of the Lord comes to and through a foreign king.[3] Abraham, the one called to walk with God, stands guilty of lying and gross mistreatment of his wife and her suitors, while the supposedly heathen locals are mortified at the thought that they might have sinned against God. Abraham's fear of mistreatment in spite of God's repeated promise that he would be blessed stands in contrast to the immediate and obedient fear of God that breaks out in the court at Gerar as soon as God speaks there. Abimelek's concern for Sarah's chastity is deeper than that of her husband, who knows that she is to bear the child of the promise. Everything is upside-down. Something, it seems, has gone horribly wrong.

> Early the next morning Abimelek summoned all his officials, and when he told them all that had happened, they were very much afraid. Then Abimelek called Abraham in and said, "What have you done to us? How have I wronged you that you have brought such great guilt upon me and my kingdom? You have done things to me that should never be done." And Abimelek asked Abraham, "What was your reason for doing this?" Abraham replied, "I said to myself, 'There is surely no fear of God in this place, and they will kill me because of my wife.'"
>
> GENESIS 20:8-11

I suggest that Abraham's failures, thrown into such sharp relief by Abimelek's God-fearing response, are failures from which we should learn, in hope that we might stop repeating them. His failures have at least four causes, all of which subvert what God had called him to be, and all of which become intertwined with cultural difference. All are factors that can similarly undermine present efforts to live faithfully in a culturally diverse world. Let's explore each one briefly.

Fear

First, there is *fear*. Both in this instance and on the other occasions when Abraham passed off his wife as his sister, fear for his safety and his future well-being is an explicit motive. Fear is one of the basic challenges of life in general — what will happen to me? Will I be kept safe amid the world's dangers? Will I have a good life? What if everything suddenly goes wrong? But in this particular instance Abraham's fear has a more specific context: God has called him to live the life of a wandering stranger, far from his home territory, outside his home culture. The first incident of self-protective lying occurred in Egypt (Genesis 12:10-20); this time Abraham is at Gerar. Both times his fear centers upon the treatment that he might receive at the hands of the locals.

> "Besides, she really is my sister, the daughter of my father though not of my mother; and she became my wife. And when God had me wander from my father's household, I said to her, 'This is how you can show your love to me: Everywhere we go, say of me, "He is my brother."'" Then Abimelek brought sheep and cattle and male and female slaves and gave them to Abraham, and he returned Sarah his wife to him. And Abimelek said, "My land is before you; live wherever you like."
>
> GENESIS 20:12-15

There is a peculiar vulnerability involved in being a stranger — a migrant, a refugee, an exile, any kind of alien.[4] Every human community has a multitude of unspoken rules about when to speak (and about what), when to be silent, where to go for what, what to call things, when to smile, what to praise, what to despise, and so on. Children of the community internalize these rules as they grow, often simply through imitation or by means of a disapproving parental stare. For the stranger, who has learned other rules and cannot rely on the locals, who are scarcely aware of their own habits, to foresee and explain all of his likely mistakes, there are daily reminders of not belonging, of being an outsider who does not quite fit in.

This sense of not being at home goes together with a certain insecurity. The stranger does not share the native's roots. The locals inhabit networks of family, clan, and other social groupings. The stranger cannot as easily call upon the support of the community; the community owes him or her no deep-grained debt of loyalty. In the extreme case, the stranger is at risk of being cheated, mistreated, deported, or even attacked. Such things happen often enough to offer a plausible basis for anxiety, and it is not necessary to cross oceans to encounter them. It is easy for the stranger to feel an exaggerated sense of fear, and hard to avoid the sense that some degree of anxiety is justified.

POWER

This already hints at a second factor in Abraham's situation: *power.* While some strangers are honored, and some locals are despised and marginalized, it is commonly those who are different who are in various ways pushed to the fringe of a community. It is clear in the present story that whatever his wealth, Abraham perceives himself as relatively powerless. Indeed, as a foreigner, Abraham *is* relatively powerless. Having no born right to be where he is, he is at the mercy of the local community's decisions about how to treat him and dependent on his own ability to defend himself if necessary. Abimelek sits secure amidst his officials, wielding institutional authority and enjoying standing among the dominant group. Abraham is an outsider, and such power as he gains here will have to be bought, or granted him by the locals. When the powerful king sends for the nomad's wife, powerlessness works with fear to keep both Abraham and Sarah silent.

Cultural differences are not just benign variations, like colors on a painter's palette; they constantly become places where power is unevenly distributed so that cultures and those who indwell them are more or less powerful, more or less vulnerable. These differences in cultural power can operate both between societies and between groups within a society. Lack of cultural power can encourage fear. Abraham might have been less tempted to defensive dishonesty if his position had seemed more secure.

At the same time as it exposes the vulnerability of the stranger, this story addresses the power of the king. When Abimelek, the powerful one, is addressed by God, he is told, despite his legitimate claim to have been wronged, to lay down his position of power before Abraham, the foreign visitor. He is to ask Abraham to intercede for him. He is to treat Abraham as a prophet and thus grant him authority, even

> To Sarah he said, "I am giving your brother a thousand shekels of silver. This is to cover the offense against you before all who are with you; you are completely vindicated." Then Abraham prayed to God, and God healed Abimelek, his wife and his female slaves so they could have children again, for the LORD had kept all the women in Abimelek's household from conceiving because of Abraham's wife Sarah.
>
> GENESIS 20:16-18

though he is a foreigner in the land and a patent liar. God calls him not only to honor and protect the stranger in his midst, but to receive from him, even though this stranger has not been good news. Other responses might have been more natural — those with power and rights tend to enjoy wielding them more than laying them down for another's good. Not all of us are kings (or politicians or executives or officials or employers), but we may wield power in other ways, perhaps simply because of the groups we belong to because of our ethnicity or education. We face the same choices. We live alongside vulnerable strangers, if we have eyes to see. Dealing with the inhabitants of Gerar would have been a more fearful thing had the one on the throne chosen to wield his power for his own convenience.

KNOWLEDGE

To fear and power we can add *partial knowledge*. Abraham's fear is not simply a product of a fevered imagination. He has past experience of local rulers taking an interest in owning his wife (Genesis 12:10-20). He has heard of bad things happening to travelers in this part of the world (compare the story of his nephew Lot and his experiences in Sodom in Genesis 19).[5] He has even witnessed firsthand God's judgment on a group of nearby cities, a judgment that fell because their wickedness was so great that not even ten righteous ones could be found (Genesis 19). Abraham thus arrives in Gerar armed with knowledge — he "knows" that no one in this place fears God, that this is a ruthless people, that they would think nothing of doing away with a foreign visitor in order to appropriate his beautiful wife. He takes what seems to him a rational course of action based on what he "knows."[6]

To a degree such "knowing" is a normal and useful part of how human thinking works. As I look out my window, I see my lawn covered with uncountable small objects, all slightly different shapes and shades of yellow and brown. I am a finite creature with finite capacities for processing information; grouping them all under the general heading "leaves" (even if more than a few should turn out to be pieces of bark or twigs) makes things much more manageable than if I were to try to hold each object's uniqueness in my mind. We do the same kind of thing all the time in order to deal with the complexity of our environment, and we cheerfully extend the habit to people. New acquaintances are quickly assigned to broad categories (young men, middle-aged women, blondes, sporty types, immigrants, academics, rednecks, foreigners, and so on) to help us keep our world straight without mental overload — and to protect our comfortable ways of organizing our world. In the process we tend to associate the ideas we have about the general category with the individual before us, regardless of whether there is any evidence in this particular case that our generalizations apply. This is stereotyping, and it is a particularly fertile source of misunderstanding and prejudice when cultural differences are in play.

Abraham "knows" what folk around here are like — but the narrative is at pains to point out that his "knowledge," in spite of its basis in recent experience, is plain wrong. He *knows* that people in this region don't fear God. And yet when God appears to Abimelek in a dream the response is prompt and humble obedience. Moreover, the narrative pauses to note that when Abimelek's court hears about the dream they too are "very much afraid." Apparently these people *do* fear God. People in this area, Abraham knows, have no respect for marriage or for the safety of a beautiful foreigner's husband. But in his dream encounter with God, Abimelek shows immediate recognition that if he had knowingly touched another man's wife it would have been a sin, and effectively protests (without contradiction from God) that if he had known Sarah was married he would not have sent for her. It even seems doubtful whether desire was his motive.

While Genesis 18:23 had Abraham asking God not to destroy the innocent (and meeting no resistance), Genesis 20:4-5 now has Abimelek making the same plea to God and casts Abraham in the role of the wicked.[7] The next day, Abimelek comes clean in public (unlike Abraham, who is still making excuses). He does not merely return Sarah to her husband, but gives her a generous gift to vindicate her reputation in the eyes of the community (thus showing significantly more concern for her chastity than Abraham himself has shown to date, and displaying a law-abiding character).[8] Apparently these people *do* respect marriage and try to do right by foreigners. Interestingly, Abimelek's outraged question when he confronts Abraham is literally "What did you see, that you would do this?" (Genesis 20:10).[9] How did Abraham see the people of Gerar? Abraham acted upon what he "knew" about this people group, and he turned out to be comprehensively mistaken. Such is often the case with what we "know" about other groups of people, and especially other cultures.[10]

PERSPECTIVE

Finally, fear, powerlessness and partial knowledge are bound up with a *limited spiritual horizon.* The story implicitly rebukes Abraham's understanding of God in two ways. First, his sense of God's presence with him and of God's faithfulness to past promises clearly still has room for growth. God has promised to bless him, to be his shield, to make his name great, and has told him not to fear (Genesis 12:1-3; 15:1). The divine invitation has been to root his identity and his future in the God who has called him, to live by faith and not by the security or insecurity of his cultural location. But Abraham is afraid and feels the need to secure his own well-being, even at the expense of his and his wife's integrity. Lack of faith gives birth to sin. Fear of God gives way to fear of others and of the future.

> The LORD had said to Abram, "Go from your country, your people, and your father's household to the land I will show you. I will make you into a great nation and I will bless you; I will make your name great, and you will be a blessing. I will bless those who bless you, and whoever curses you I will curse; and all peoples on earth will be blessed through you."
>
> GENESIS 12:1-3

At the same time, paradoxically, Abraham seems to think of God as located with him but not among the Philistines. *They* don't fear God (implying that *I* do). This is a godless place where the godly (the group to which *I* belong) are at risk. This perspective is sharply exposed in the narrative. God speaks not to Abraham, the prophet, but to Abimelek, the heathen. Fear of God and obedience to God are found not in Abraham's household, but among the supposedly godless inhabitants of Gerar.[11] When Abraham arrives in the area he does not reckon on God already being there; once again he is mistaken.

As with the other factors discussed above, this one seems disturbingly normal if we pause to look around and within. One of my college students, when asked on a questionnaire why Christians should take an interest in other languages, once wrote, "They should because if they don't then people who do not know English will not hear the gospel." We may smile at this as naïve, but it merely states baldly a common subconscious assumption. It goes like this: God is with me, God works and speaks in my culture (despite its defects), and if I take the risk of venturing into other cultures I bring God with me; I have little expectation that God is saying things to members of the other culture that I need to hear, or that *they* will teach *me* obedience or challenge *my* sin. God speaks my language and likes my ways, and must surely share my discomfort at the strange ways of others. If we assume that there is none of this attitude in us, it may be because we have never ventured far enough from home to be put to the test. The standard human tendency is to declare that the earth is the Lord's but to locate his favorite chair in my own backyard.

> The earth is the LORD's, and everything in it, the world, and all who live in it; for he founded it on the seas and established it on the waters.
>
> PSALM 24:1-2

These four factors working together — fear, power (and lack of power), partial knowledge, and limited spiritual horizons — lead to an unsettling result: Abraham achieves the opposite of that for which he was called. When first addressing Abraham (then called Abram), God defined his future in terms of bringing blessing to all the peoples of the earth. More than that, Abraham was to "*be* a blessing" — he was to grow in such a way that his presence would be a channel of well-being. Here in Gerar (as in that other episode among the Egyptians) he brings dishonesty and subterfuge that lead his hosts into judgment and fear of death.[12] In place of thanks for blessings received, the response is, "What did we do to you to deserve this? What could have been going through your mind that you would treat us like this?" This is hardly a prime instance of being a blessing.

Cultural differences have been with us since before the time of Abraham, and so has the challenge of communicating with integrity across cultural fault lines. What makes this an issue of growing urgency in our day is the exponential increase in contact between cultures. Efficient and relatively inexpensive means of global transport mean that increasing numbers of people can pay brief visits to the other side of the world. Through the media of communication such as television, telephones, and the Internet we can be placed in contact with another culture in seconds, enjoying the illusion of instant access and fallen barriers. And the towns and cities where most people live and work are themselves densely and increasingly multicultural. The other side of the world may, in cultural terms, be just across the street. The chances of spending the rest of my life solely in contact with people who are culturally like me are increasingly slim. As Abraham's story shows, however, mere contact is no guarantee of learning, peace, or blessing. As contact grows, so does the opportunity for both good and evil, for both blessing and cursing.

If our reactions to cultural difference have such potential to turn a desire to bless into the ability to curse, then we can ill afford ignorance about culture and its effects upon us and our callings. Is it possible to be a blessing in spite of cultural differences? Only if some important learning takes place. Learning the dynamics of cultural difference can no longer be a special training restricted to missionaries. It is a necessary part of the learning that any disciple of Christ who desires to "be a blessing" to those outside his or her immediate clan must undergo. The alternative is to walk a little too thoroughly in Abraham's footsteps.

CHAPTER 2

CULTURE AND BAD BREATH

T ry the following thought experiment: close your eyes (after reading the rest of this paragraph!) and imagine a person who is from a culture that is different from your own. It could be someone you know or a total stranger — the main thing is that they are from another culture. Try to picture them in your mind's eye as clearly and in as much detail as you can. Take a few moments to do that now, before you read further.

Now take a mental step back and consider what kinds of things came to mind. Did you imagine someone with different facial features, or a different skin color — say, for instance, a Chinese face (if you are

African) or a European face (if you are Native American) or an Indian face (if you are of European extraction)? Did you imagine different clothing, perhaps with different colors and fabrics? Perhaps (if you managed to sketch in the details) you saw an unusual hairstyle or distinctive jewelry?

Now consider my experience as an Englishman currently living in the American Midwest. Take, for example, the day when I took the bus to pick up my car, which was undergoing some needed repairs. Unsure of the exact location of the nearest bus stop, I pressed the button to ask the driver to halt as we approached the repair shop where my car was waiting. I then stood up and moved to the front of the bus. About fifty yards further along the street the driver opened the front door of the bus and slowed to a stop. I descended the steps and got out — and was taken aback to find the bus driver yelling at me in anger. It turned out that he had not stopped to let me out; he had stopped because of a railroad crossing. Buses in the city where I live stop and open the door to look for trains before proceeding across a railroad crossing. Buses in England do not do that (and more rarely have to cross train tracks). Not knowing the custom, I innocently got off the bus at a place where I was forbidden to do so. And I made an enemy, at least for a few minutes, of a bus driver whom I had never met.

It is not hard to multiply examples of the discomfort that stems from not being tuned in to local assumptions. I am used to a more reserved form of public interaction in England and was quite taken aback the first time a supermarket employee, a total stranger, greeted me and asked me how I was doing. The first thought to run through my mind was: Who are you? What are you trying to get from me? Not being used to having young women look me in the eye and smile as I walked past them (that would almost be an invitation where I come from), I wondered if moving to Michigan had mysteriously made me more attractive overnight. Being used to wearing "trousers" and to using the word "pants" to refer to underwear, I was reduced to a state of some confusion when someone pointed out that I had my pants caught in my sock. I still, after several years, find it mildly disconcerting that even colleagues whom I do not know well continually use my first name, even when exchanging fleeting greetings in the hallways; this is not the norm where I come from. Recently I was suffused with a burst of irrational joy when, after months of hearing "Hi, how're you doing?" as I passed people, a British colleague greeted me with "Hello, nice weather we're having" — at last, someone greeted me the right way! The list could go on for quite some time.

What does this have to do with our thought experiment? I am white and European and work at a college at which white folk of European descent are in the majority. I speak English (albeit with an accent that identifies me as foreign every time I open my mouth); the people around me speak English. My choice of clothes falls pretty much within the normal range seen around campus. My hairstyle is unexceptional, and I don't wear jewelry. And yet I am daily reminded that I am not in my home culture. There are a great number of small, unwritten, unnoticed rules of social behavior that generate a frequently renewed sense of not quite fitting in my new environment. My appearance is unremarkable; various cultural aspects of my identity, my assumptions, and my expectations were, however, shaped elsewhere.

It is tempting when we begin to think about culture to focus mainly on the visible (think back: what appeared in your mind's eye when you imagined someone from another culture?) — on outward markers of ethnicity. But those things may not be the real location of cultural difference (it is possible for me to be of the same culture as someone with a different skin tone, and to differ in culture from someone who looks just like me), and even when they do indicate cultural difference, they are the tip of the iceberg. The most interesting differences are invisible until we begin to interact.

They are especially invisible to ourselves. What almost always strikes me first when various cultural frictions arise is how odd U.S. culture seems, rather than how strange I am. It is, no doubt, my North American friends who look at me and raise a mental eyebrow. This is a standard part of how people tend to operate. Culture is a little like bad breath — you tend to notice it in other people sooner than you detect it in yourself. Africans dancing to tribal drums have culture; Indians singing to the sound of a sitar have culture; Maori sticking out their tongues, Japanese folk bowing, Inuit building igloos, and Englishmen playing cricket: all of these are obviously cultural behaviors — unless you happen to be part of one of these cultures. When we look at ourselves, we tend to imagine that we see normality, life as it should be (give or take a few personal idiosyncrasies). We take it for granted that we can communicate with others, that our humor is understood, that our appearance causes no alarm, and that our decisions and choices make sense. We are normal; others are different, perhaps even exotic. We measure their degree of "strangeness" against our own sense of normality — such is our subconscious way of ordering things (like the apocryphal British lady who, while visiting a far-off land, was faced with the choice between two lanes at passport control, one labeled "foreigners" and the other "nationals." She is fabled to have chosen the latter, on the grounds that she "certainly wasn't a foreigner!").

The Complexity of "Normal"

"Normal," however, has a habit of getting more complex if you look at it more closely. Consider the following description of a U.S. citizen's morning routine, written in 1936:

> Our solid American citizen awakens in a bed built on a pattern which originated in the Near East but which was modified in Northern Europe before it was transmitted to America. He throws back covers made from cotton, domesticated in India, or silk, the use of which was discovered in China. . . . He slips into his moccasins, invented by the Indians of the Eastern woodlands, and goes to the bathroom. . . . He takes off his pajamas, a garment invented in India, and washes with soap invented by the ancient Gauls. He then shaves, a masochistic rite which seems to have been derived from either Sumer or ancient Egypt.
>
> Returning to the bedroom, . . . [h]e puts on garments whose form originally derived from the skin clothing of the nomads of the Asiatic steppes, puts on shoes made from skins tanned by a process invented in ancient Egypt and cut to a pattern derived from the classical civilization of the Mediterranean, and ties around his neck a strip of bright-colored cloth which is a vestigial survival of shoulder shawls worn by the seventeenth-century Croatians. Before going out for breakfast he glances through the window, made out of glass invented in Egypt, and if it is raining . . . takes an umbrella, invented in southeastern Asia.
>
> On the way to breakfast he stops to buy a paper, paying for it with coins, an ancient Lydian invention. At the restaurant . . . [h]is

plate is made of a form of pottery invented in China. His knife is of steel, an alloy first made in southern India, his fork a medieval Italian invention, and his spoon a derivative of a Roman original . . . he may have an egg of a species of bird domesticated in Indo-China, or thin strips of the flesh of an animal domesticated in East Asia which have been salted and smoked by a process developed in northern Europe.

When our friend has finished eating he . . . reads the news of the day, imprinted in characters invented by the ancient Semites upon a material invented in China by a process invented in Germany. As he absorbs the accounts of foreign troubles he will, if he is a good conservative citizen, thank a Hebrew deity in an Indo-European language that he is 100 per cent American.[1]

What was already true in 1936 is still truer now: the everyday artifacts that surround us from dawn to dusk are the products of a wide array of different cultures spanning the globe and the centuries. Cultural diversity is not just "out there" in other people — you and your daily behaviors are already bound up in it. Your ordinary, everyday self is a cultural mosaic.

Now, this is all kind of entertaining if you have any interest in cultural history, but so what? You should succeed in getting your food to your mouth regardless of whether you know where the implements came from. We need to take a step further, because culture affects more than your clothing or eating habits. It also affects the way that you experience the world around you, because culture is not just a question of different behaviors, but also of the meanings that we assign to things. It affects, for example, the way that you hear.

HEARING DIFFICULTIES

In a book about his experiences among the Motilone Indians of Venezuela, missionary writer Bruce Olson reports his first meeting with the natives of the upper reaches of the Orinoco River. Christian missionaries had been at work among the Indians, but they told him that their new converts were being persecuted by the rest of the tribe. Olson went to talk to the other Indians. They found the notion of persecution ridiculous and instead complained that the converts to Christianity among their tribe did not care about them anymore. When he asked why, they told him:

> Why, they've rejected everything about us. . . . They won't sing our songs now. They sing those weird, wailing songs that are all out of tune and don't make sense. And the construction which they call a church! Have you seen their church? It's square! How can God be in a square church? Round is perfect. . . . It has no ending, like God. But the Christians, their God has points all over, bristling at us. And how those Christians dress! Such foolish clothes. . . .[2]

The Christian converts had been taught North American hymns, on the assumption that these sounded inherently religious and were somehow intrinsically conducive to worship. To the locals, with their very different musical culture, they did not sound religious; they sounded weird, wailing, and senseless.

Similar issues arise much closer to home. The following lament is drawn from an article by a North American Christian college professor:

> During their high school days many . . . students have had a weeklong "mission" trip to a country in Latin America. Prior to the trip they studied little about the culture or the church that exists in that country so that they might learn from them. It is even more disconcerting that when they were there they were happiest not when experiencing authentic expressions of national culture, but when they found a McDonalds or a Pizza Hut, when they presented a drama or pantomime originally designed for a North American youth culture audience, or when they sang "American" Christian songs that had been translated into Spanish or Portuguese.[3]

We easily (and incorrectly) assume that sounds that we have learned to associate, say, with church (whether that is organs, choirs, or guitars; classical, gospel, or contemporary worship songs) are somehow naturally connected with Christian piety.[4] Such connections are, however, culturally learned, and anyone who has ever experienced tension with their parents concerning their musical tastes knows how even the slight differences in aural culture that exist between generations of the same family can result in two people registering the same sounds with their ears but apparently hearing quite different things.

HOME-TINTED SPECTACLES

So culture affects how you hear. It also affects how you see. Contrary to popular belief, what you see is not what you get — what we see when we look at things is embedded in the expectations, concepts, and interpretive frames that we have learned to apply. This is a common theme in psychological studies of perception:

> [P]rior experience may often set up "expectancies" that cause us to "see" what is not there, as the following true story illustrates. A woman shopping for groceries hears a young child scream, "Stop, stop, you're killing my father." She turns the corner to see a very large man on top of another man choking him, with blood all around the victim's head. She runs for help, thinking she has witnessed a murderous assault. When she returns several minutes later she discovers that the "murder" she would have sworn in court she saw was not a murder at all. A man had an epileptic seizure and fell, hitting and cutting his head. A second man had tried to prevent further injury to the first man by loosening the man's tie and holding his head up. The woman realized on her second look that there was only a small amount of blood from the quite minor cut, and even more amazing was her realization that the vicious, huge "man on top" was a neighbor of hers, actually small of stature.[5]

What we see is conditioned by cultural learning. An Asian tourist once stopped me in a street in Oxford, pointed to the yellow lines along the side of the road that signaled that parking was forbidden, and asked if those lines would give her a tour of the university if she followed them — a bizarre question to me, but an innocent one to her. We were looking at the same yellow paint but not seeing the same thing. When we observe behaviors, images, films, works of art, and the many other artifacts of another culture we are often very poorly placed to know what is actually in front of our eyes. (You see, for instance, a man kiss another man — what does it mean? The answer depends a great deal on the cultural setting.) When I hear students from my college on a visit to Germany comment that medieval Lübeck looks "like an outdoor mall," I have fresh evidence that we tend to see the world through our own cultural spectacles.

Given the human tendency to arrive swiftly at judgments of quality and moral worth based on initial impressions, this provides plenty of temptation to make hasty but inappropriate evaluations about that which is culturally other. We can become deeply attached to our particular way of seeing, especially when questions of identity seem to be at stake, even if the images that we have formed are clearly biased. Those, for instance, who since childhood have seen Jesus portrayed in storybooks as white with flowing hair can become unreasonably disturbed if told that he was more likely olive-skinned with short, dark curls.[6] We have learned to see, with our physical eyes and with our mind's eye, as members of a culture, and learning to see in other ways can be a struggle.

TALKING PAST ONE ANOTHER

Hearing, seeing — what about speaking? Culture deeply affects the way you speak and your chances of making yourself understood. When communication is flowing well, it's easy not to notice language, or to think of it as a simple postal system whereby your thoughts are packed into words and the words ferry them safely across to the other person's mind, where they are unpacked in good shape, undamaged by the journey. But this is wide of the mark. French thinker Jacques Ellul points out that words are fuzzy, that they are surrounded by an imprecise cloud of associations. He says:

> Even the simplest word — bread, for instance — . . . calls up many images which form a dazzling rainbow, a multitude of echoes. When the word bread is pronounced, I cannot help but think of the millions of people who have none. I cannot avoid the image of a certain baker friend of mine, and of the time during the Nazi occupation when bread was so scarce and of such poor quality. The communion service comes to me . . . [and] the moral lessons I learned as a child: that it is a crime to throw away a piece of bread,

since it is a sacred substance. . . . Memories come back to me: the warm, crusty bread of my childhood. The promised bread of life that will satisfy all hunger. And not living by bread alone. . . . Not all of these memories are conjured up every time I hear the word, and they do not all come at once, but it is a rarity when none of them follows the oft-repeated request: "pass me the bread."[7]

Words carry a rich halo of cultural references and reminiscences. This means that when I talk to someone whose experiences and feelings do not match my own, my words may not convey to them precisely what they convey to me. I may get my basic message across, but my chances of full and precise communication are reduced where there is cultural difference. This is one reason why jokes often fall flat when lobbed across cultural lines, and it can lead to embarrassing mistakes. Once, when I lived in Germany, I made a comment to my landlady about my particularly busy day. I said, *"Heute wollte jeder etwas von mir"* — literally, "Today everyone wanted something from me." It was only a couple of days later that I discovered that the phrase to "want something from someone" was a local euphemism for unwanted sexual attention.

The connection between culture and communication does not stop there. Culture inhabits not only your words, but even the spaces between them. At a conference on Native American education in Albuquerque, New Mexico, some years ago there was a small group session involving some Navajo teachers. It was supposed to have been a discussion of educational problems in their schools, but to the disappointment of the organizers none of the teachers had talked. All were educators, all had come because of their interest in the topic, so what could have gone wrong? Muriel Saville-Troike, a sociolinguist, set out to investigate, and came to believe that cultural factors had played a large role. She tells of visiting a kindergarten class located on the Navajo reservation, and seeing a Navajo man open the classroom door as class was in progress and stand in silence, looking at the floor. The teacher was Anglo-American, and said, "Good morning," to the Navajo visitor. She expected some kind of response, but received none, so she introduced herself and than waited once more, again encountering silence. At this point the teacher noticed one of her students putting away his things and fetching his coat, and she asked the man if he was taking his son. "Yes," he responded, the only word he contributed to the conversation, even though the teacher continued to talk to him until the pair left. Saville-Troike relates:

> The teacher shrugged her shoulders at me, conveying helplessness and frustration. From a Navajo perspective, the man's silence was appropriate and respectful. The teacher, on the other hand, expected not only to have the man return her greeting, but to have him identify himself and state his reason for being there. This would have required the man to break not only Navajo rules of politeness but also a traditional religious taboo that prohibits individuals from saying their own name. The teacher engaged in small talk in an attempt to be friendly and to cover her discomfort in the situation, as appropriate in her own speech community, while the man continued to maintain the silence appropriate in his.[8]

Saville-Troike suggests that these differences might help explain what happened at the conference in Albuquerque. The dynamics at the conference were no doubt complex, perhaps affected by resentments rooted in the troubled history of interactions between Navajo and Anglo-Americans. Yet it seems that it was at least in part these Navajo rules of politeness that undermined the group session. The discussion leader had asked questions, and the Navajo participants had naturally observed respectful silences before offering an answer. Anglo-Americans have a fairly low level of tolerance for stretches of silence in a discussion, and so tended to dominate. The Navajo were apparently kept out of the discussion by what they saw as an impolite failure to observe sufficient pauses for them to answer respectfully. Each side found the other side's behavior impolite and frustrating. Here we have a group of people with a lot in common — all educators, all speaking English — yet utterly failing to communicate because of an unidentified cultural difference. Notice that it was not the words that blocked communication — everyone spoke English — but the length of the spaces between them. Even silences can convey cultural meaning.

Behaving Yourself in Public

Finally, all of these forms of culturally loaded perception (and more) feed into, and are reinforced by, the ways that we behave. The whole spectrum of human perceptions and behaviors turns out to be influenced by culture. One might think, for example, that the way that people behave when under the influence of alcohol is pretty much a matter of biochemical effects. Chemicals and their effects on the human body are clearly involved. Cross-cultural studies of the effects of alcohol suggest, however, that behaviors resulting from alcohol consumption vary widely across cultures, and drinkers tend to adopt the behaviors that their culture associates with being under the influence of alcohol. In some countries (such as the U.S., Great Britain, and Australia) the consumption of alcohol is associated with aggressive and antisocial behavior; in others (such as Latin American and Mediterranean nations) the same dose of alcohol generally yields calmness and peaceful good humor.[9] Perhaps most interesting are studies in which individuals are given nonalcoholic drinks but led to believe that they are alcoholic. The individuals involved begin to exhibit the behaviors that their culture associates with drunkenness.[10] Our behaviors are conditioned by what we believe is expected and normal, and we learn those expectations from our culture.

In our day-to-day living we neither enact nor encounter a random collection of individual behaviors. Rather, we insert ourselves into more complex interlocking patterns of behavior. Consider as an example the commonplace act of eating out.[11] Take a few minutes to imagine yourself going out for a meal with friends — not to a fast food place or anything too fancy, just an ordinary, run-of-the-mill restaurant that you know. Think through each part of the process and jot down what happens:

1. *Arriving at the restaurant.* (How do you get there? Where is the restaurant? What interactions take place before you end up seated ready to eat?)
2. *Ordering your meal.* (How are food options presented to you? How does the person serving the food behave? What interactions are expected? What do you expect to be included?)
3. *Eating your meal.* (What happens during the eating of the meal? How long does the meal last?)

4. *Concluding the meal.* (What are the steps that lead to payment for the meal? How do you pay? What happens to leftovers? When do you leave?)

Now take a few moments to consider what cultural values are expressed in the behaviors that you described, and which of the interactions that you listed might seem strange to someone from a different culture.

Every stage in the process is culturally loaded (even your digestion may be affected by your lifestyle). Consider the possible experiences of foreign visitors to a restaurant in the United States. Not every restaurant or customer from a given culture is identical — but the description that follows does represent some general differences between mainstream North American expectations and those in other parts of the world.

Our first visitors, a German couple, are impressed by the amount of parking space around the restaurant, being more used to parking some distance away and walking, perhaps through a pedestrianized area of the city. On arriving at the restaurant, their natural inclination would be to walk in, choose a table, and seat themselves; if the restaurant were very full, but some of the occupied tables had empty seats, they might find it normal to ask those already seated if the empty seats were free and join their table. But they notice the prominent "Please Wait to be Seated" sign and wait dutifully. From here on in, however, there is considerably less waiting than they are used to. An employee appears, says, "Two?" (they deduce that this must refer to them and nod), leads them to a table, and assures them that their server will be along swiftly. Instead of having (as in Germany) to catch the attention of a passing waiter in order to be served, they find that one quickly appears and behaves to their perception more like a long-lost friend than a waiter, greeting them warmly and telling them (rather irrelevantly) his first name. He also brings them water that they didn't order and then asks them if they would like anything to drink — an odd sequence to people who would normally never drink water from a faucet in a restaurant, would order carbonated bottled water if that were what they wanted, and would not expect any drink to be complimentary. They order Cokes and a meal, and are surprised (despite the refrain of reassurances from the server that any request will "be right out") at how quickly the food comes. They are also surprised (and a little irritated) at how often the server returns to their table to interrupt them with questions about how they are doing. They are even more surprised when he whisks their drinks away before they have finished drinking them and quickly replaces them with fresh ones that they did not order — free refills are not the norm in Germany, drinks can be expensive there, and anyway, the first drinks that they were given were enormous. The general sense of speed is reinforced to an almost offensive degree when the bill appears on the table before they ask for it — before they have even quite finished eating; is this establishment that keen to get rid of them? And why would they want a box? Surely this person does not think that they are so poor as to have no food at home? It would never have occurred to them to ask for the leftovers for later. Fortunately, they have been forewarned about tipping, but they still feel a little resentful at the size of the tip — back home, service is included and the tip is usually small change. Before an hour has passed, they find themselves outside again — in Germany they might have sat and talked long after the eating was done, but here the implicit assumption (communicated through the swift removal of plates, presenting of the check, and inquiry as to whether that will be all) seems to be that they should leave as soon as they have finished eating.

As our German guests leave, a small group of Chinese tourists enters.[12] They share some of the specific puzzlements of the German couple — the iced water, the over-friendly server, the frequent visits to the table, the tipping, the discouragement of lingering after the meal — but also have some of their own. They are surprised to see that the tables are rectangular instead of the round tables to which they are accustomed. They also find it quite odd that smoking is prohibited and feel that the background music is a little intrusive. They resigned themselves ahead of time to eating with awkward implements such as knives and forks, but are taken aback at being given individual menus and being expected to order individually. Normally only the host, who will be treating the others, is given the menu and will order a range of dishes that "we" will have on behalf of the entire group. The dishes will be shared by everyone, people will pour and refill each other's drinks rather than their own, and only one person will pay. In such a group of friends, whoever pays for everyone will know that the next time (which will certainly occur, given the strength of Chinese friendships) someone else in the group will take a turn at paying. When the food comes, they discuss its lack of variety — the over-dominance of meat, lack of vegetables, bland flavors, and the way everything is overcooked, so that the vegetables "have no soul left." They would prefer to enjoy a beer with their meal and are disappointed with sickeningly sweet cola or freezing cold ice water as a substitute (cold drinks do not go with hot food!). The host is happy that there is food left at the end — it shows that he generously provided enough to satisfy his guests — and does not see the need to take the remaining food home. When time for dessert comes, there is little interest — back home they do not usually eat dessert, and the American desserts are way too sweet and could feed a family of four.

The differences between the cultures that our sample visitors represent and the culture of the typical North American restaurant are not absolute — there are overlaps, and it is possible for each visitor to get through the experience. Nevertheless, at every turn something feels slightly askew. The North American restaurant setting has its own particular interlocking pattern of behaviors, and the pattern is no accident. It is infused with values that are strongly embedded in the wider culture, such as speed, efficiency and control (controlling the flow of people, designating where customers sit, moving them rapidly through the stages of the meal, checking progress regularly), individualism (individual menus and plates, asking whether the meal will be paid for separately), public informality and a related understanding of customer service (introduction by first name, demonstrative friendliness, frequent chatty interactions), an association between pleasure and quantity of consumption (portion sizes, frequent drink refills), and the importance of value for money (keeping some visible elements of the meal out of the price, free refills, separating the meal cost from the service charge).

The German restaurant experience is not opposed in every respect to these values, but does not map cleanly onto them either. It is more strongly shaped by values such as public formality (more formal interaction with the waiter, less intrusion into personal space during the meal), guarding of time for leisure and personal relationships (more time spent over the meal and talking afterwards), and paying one's dues (no free refills, the full cost advertised up front).

The Chinese visitors bring a further set of values and expectations — an orientation toward the welfare of the group rather than that of the individual (paying and ordering collectively, sharing the food from each dish, round tables), a focus on hospitality and generosity (pouring drinks for one another, making sure there is plenty of food), and an emphasis on long-term relationship rather than efficient encounters (taking turns to pay, lingering sociably over food).

While the differences can be listed as a series of individual behaviors, what is most culturally telling (and often hardest to become consciously aware of when one is an insider to a cultural setting) is not the individual actions, but the larger pattern of meanings that is in play, and the ways in which this pattern (more than individual exceptions and variations) reflects shared beliefs, assumptions, commitments, and values. Restaurant behavior is just one example. We live out our lives by means of such cultural patterns and the behavioral settings that they support, enacting more or less gracefully the roles that they provide for us (the polite customer, the attentive waitress), and for the most part assuming that they are "normal." We may even get very offended when the pattern is broken — if, say, the waiter fails to bring us a menu or is slow with the check. When someone offends against the pattern, it can feel like an offense against our very self.

This is in one sense simply the way it has to be. Without cultural patterns, there would be no culture — we would not have restaurants, payment systems, or the experience of eating out. Living in a culture is the price of being human; the alternative is to live at the level of instinct and biological necessity. At the same time, however, conscious awareness of the patterned nature of our lives can be disturbing. What if we are uncomfortable with the values shaping our culture and our sense of self? How much room do we have to resist if our very perceptions are already culturally loaded? And what does it mean to live a life rooted in Christ if so much of our way of life simply reflects the assumptions of our society? Realizing that culture goes much deeper than a few differences in dress, dance, or music leads directly to such questions, and requires us to consider whether culture is a cage and what kind of responsibility it leaves to us.

CHAPTER 3

CAGE, CARNIVAL, OR CALLING?

Suppose you were asked to write a spiritual autobiography, an account of God's ways with you and of how the grace you have received has shaped you over the course of your life. Where would you start? What episode in your past would begin the story of your spiritual formation? Take a few moments to consider your answer before you read further.

As a modern, Western person, I find that it comes naturally to me to think of myself primarily in terms of my own individual thoughts and choices. My first inclination would be to begin the story of my spiritual life no earlier than my earliest conscious memories (even assuming I thought back that far, and did not begin much, much later with my first explicit struggles with questions of faith). I would tell what we might call an "I-story," one in which I am the subject of all the important verbs.

St. Augustine's *Confessions,* composed at the end of the fourth century A.D. by the famous North African bishop, is one of the most important spiritual autobiographies ever written. When I first read the work, I was struck by the contrast with how I would have started. Augustine begins with God, and with the ways in which God overflows our words and concepts. When he gets to himself, Augustine starts with the question of where he came from in the first place, and how he came to be a person at all. He introduces himself as a helpless infant:

> I do not know where I came from. But the consolations of your mercies upheld me (cf. Ps. 50:3; 93:19), as I have heard from the parents of my flesh, him from whom and her in whom you formed me in time. For I do not remember. So I was welcomed by the consolations of human milk. . . . Indeed all good things come from you, O God, and 'from God is all my salvation' (2 Sam. 23:5). I became aware of this only later when you cried aloud to me through the gifts which you bestow both inwardly in mind and outwardly in body. For at that time I knew nothing more than how to suck and to be quietened by bodily delights, and to weep when I was physically uncomfortable.[1]

Augustine realizes that his life as someone who could receive gifts and respond to those who gave them started further back than his conscious memories, back when all he could do was wriggle and suck. He goes on to ponder even earlier times, wondering about the time before his birth: "What was going on before that, my sweetness, my God? Was I anywhere or any sort of person? I have no one able to tell me that."[2] In other words, he starts his tale with the clear recognition that before he could understand or contribute anything, he was the helpless recipient of the gift of existence itself, and then of further gifts of creation — milk, kindness, human company. His way of telling his story implies that we do not hold our lives entirely within the grasp of our conscious self-awareness. Our selves are not in our own hands. Our stories are more than I-stories.

The same goes for our cultural selves. The cultural patterns that shape how we perceive, communicate, and behave were for the most part around before we arrived on the scene. They form the matrix within which we grow up. Chapter 2 considered some of the many ways in which our behavior reflects our culture. This chapter will look more closely at how culture shapes our individual trajectories through life, and will consider how we might respond to realizing how we are formed. Can the cultural patterns that precede us and shape us be regarded as gifts? Should they be resisted as cages that rob us of our freedom? Are we called to respond in particular ways? Do we have any say in the matter?

CULTURAL BEGINNINGS

Our cultural life stories, like our spiritual life stories, start before our earliest memories. The culture into which we are born has a history stretching back far before the point at which we joined it. It is not given to us as individuals to make up the words that we learn, the manners that we master, or even the kinds of dreams that we come to pursue. (British children do not usually dream of becoming baseball stars, and few North American children aspire to own camels.) The conversation started before we joined it, and we have to learn how to take our turn.[3]

Even our entry into the cultural conversation starts further back than we can remember. Research carried out with infants suggests that our cultural formation begins very early indeed. In one study, pregnant women were asked to read the same story aloud each day during the last six weeks of their pregnancies.[4] Soon after the babies were born, they were given rubber teats to suck on that were connected to a pressure-sensitive device able to detect when and how fast they sucked. This was, in turn, connected to a computer in such a way that the babies could trigger a recording of the story that the mother had been reading, sometimes by sucking faster and sometimes by sucking slower than normal. They could also hear a new story by changing their sucking speed in the opposite direction. The babies in the experiment sucked whichever way would let them hear the familiar story. Similar

experiments showed that four-day-old babies were able to discriminate between two different languages, and express a preference for the
language spoken by their mothers. Even babies still in the womb (this
time studied through measurements of fetal heart rate) responded differently to the familiar and the unfamiliar story.

Obviously, these infants were not decoding the words and admiring the plot. Word meanings are, however, not the only things going on
in language. Try saying aloud to yourself, in the tone of voice you would
use to read to a small child:

"Once upon a time there was a girl called Goldilocks,"

and then:

"It was a dark and stormy night."

Now try humming the same sentences with your lips closed, but keeping the same rhythm and the same rising and falling tone, the "melody"
of the sentence. Even without words, you can still tell that the sentences are different. These rhythms and melodies differ both between
utterances and between language varieties. Even within the English
language, for instance, speakers in some regions end statements on a
falling tone, while others end them on a rising tone (making them
sound like questions to speakers of the first group). Move into a different language or dialect and you will find a whole new set of patterns.[5] It
was the soundscape of their mothers' utterances that the infants in the
studies just described were hearing, and then responding to as something comfortingly familiar when they heard it again. Even before birth,
it seems, we have already begun to be shaped into patterns of preference for some ways of speaking over others. Already in the womb we
have begun to be groomed for living in one community rather than another.[6]

This is, of course, a very slight degree of cultural formation, but it
represents the first steps in a process that accelerates rapidly after we
are born, teaching us how to think, see, hear, behave, and dream within
the weave of a particular cultural context. As babies we may be
wrapped tight and carried around out of doors, or given space inside a
certain kind of home and encouraged to explore, or set down in front of

a television. As soon as we become able to act on our environments we begin to find some actions encouraged and others discouraged. We learn to wear the clothes considered appropriate for our age, gender, and subculture; we listen to a selection from the styles of music that our community listens to; eat the foods that our elders are accustomed to eating; and arrange our time around culturally sanctioned activities ranging from play with building blocks to organized sports, from chewing on blankets to graduate study, from watching colored lights on the nursery ceiling to rooting for Frodo as he enters Mordor. As we learn to speak, we learn not only the meanings that our culture assigns to certain sounds, but also what we can and cannot talk about in particular settings (or at all), and a host of evaluative associations attached to particular words. We learn, for instance, that certain sound combinations have obscene connotations, and we learn in ways that go far beyond the dictionary definition what it means to be "liberal," or "dogmatic," or "religious," or "nice," so that the words in our mouths taste of the ways in which others have used them.[7] In these and many more ways, our identity is increasingly interwoven with our cultural location. Our shared human nature, with its inbuilt capacities for developing language, thought, and a moral and spiritual sense, underwrites the whole process. Together with the common experiences and constraints built into life on earth, this shared humanness keeps us from being utterly alien to one another across cultural lines. However, the particular ways in which these capacities are developed and exercised owes a great deal to cultural location.

Growing up Cultured

Much of the way of life that surrounds us as infants is simply internalized as "normal," without conscious reflection on questions of goodness or badness. It is not too long, however, before we begin (often with parental assistance) to understand many of the actions being presented to us as "good" or "bad." Children growing up in homes where knives and forks are the norm are not generally told that using a fork is considered polite in this particular cultural group but seems strange to others; they are simply admonished not to eat with their fingers (and may later feel that those whose culture differs on this point are uncouth).

The cultural variations in the ways in which parents treat, talk to, discipline, and play with children are illustrated by a study carried out by developmental psychologists in the homes of Japanese and North American parents of children aged six months to nineteen months:

> They asked the mothers to clear away the toys from a play area and then introduced several that they had brought with them — a stuffed dog and pig and a car and truck. They asked the mothers to play with the toys with their babies as they normally would. They found big differences in the behavior of mothers even with their youngest children. American mothers used twice as many object labels as Japanese mothers ("piggie," "doggie") and Japanese mothers engaged in twice as many social routines of teaching politeness norms (empathy and greetings, for example). An American mother's patter might go like this: "That's a car. See the car? You like it? It's got nice wheels." A Japanese mother might say: "Here! It's a vroom vroom. I give it to you. Now give this to me. Yes! Thank you." American children are learning that the world is mostly a place with objects, Japanese children that the world is mostly about relationships.[8]

These ways of seeing and acting upon the world are usually implicit, unconscious, and unplanned for both parent and child. They are nonetheless deeply formative. They are not just arbitrary quirks of individual families, but reflect larger cultural patterns of meaning. Mainstream North American culture values self-reliance highly and is on the whole more oriented toward approaching the world as a set of objects that have fixed properties and can be manipulated without strong reference to their context, whereas many Asian cultures tend to see things much more in terms of relationships, obligations, and particular contexts.[9]

The ways in which parents and communities behave reproduce and sustain these cultural differences (with slight, cumulative modifications) across generations. Japanese mothers, when talking to their children, ask fewer questions on average about objects than their North American counterparts, and are more likely to use words associated with feelings when children misbehave, offering comments such as, "The toy is crying because you threw it." Later, in history classes at school, learning causes of events tends to be emphasized more in

North American schools, while learning to empathize with historical figures and situations carries more prominence in Japanese classrooms. Through layer upon layer of similar day-to-day processes, the self and its ways are shaped. When four- and six-year-old U.S. and Chinese children were asked to report on the events of the day, Chinese children made three times fewer references to themselves than American children did. It has been suggested that while individuals vary considerably, on average, "Asians are more acutely aware of the feelings and attitudes of others than are Westerners."[10]

While a great deal of the formation process occurs during childhood, the shaping effects of our cultural context (and the cultural self that it has given us) do not go away as we mature. Consider a mainstream North American college classroom (if this is not your context, you might find it interesting to think of how this paragraph might change for the context in which you work). Why in each case do students not normally do the following:

- Bow to their professor at the start of class?
- Sit on the floor?
- Make a point of shaking the professor's hand and thanking her for the class on the way out?
- Begin reading the assigned text from the back of the book, or read each page starting at the bottom?
- Wear suits and ties?
- Explain that the solution to the problem was revealed to them in a dream in answer to prayer?
- Stand to attention each time they answer a question?
- Burst into tears, do an uncontrolled dance, and hug the professor when they answer a question correctly?
- Interrupt the class discussion to offer an opinion about a friend's new hairstyle?

It is extremely unlikely that the college has any written rules against any of these behaviors, or that the students have heard or read any explicit admonition to avoid them (have you heard a teacher say, "Please do not wear a tie to class" at the start of the semester?). All of them are entirely appropriate in different social or cultural settings (can you think of settings in which each would make sense?). North

American students know, however, in a way that is not consciously formulated, that this is not the right way to behave in *this* setting. Each possible behavior carries symbolic significance in a given setting — it might, for instance, count as being rude, or being overly formal. We know how a classroom is different from, say, a quiz show, even if we have never considered the matter, and for the most part we follow the implicit rules that govern what messages our behaviors send in a college classroom. The main sanction keeping us within the bounds of appropriateness is embarrassment — the uncomfortable awareness of incurring the disapproval of other members of our cultural group, of not having behaved "normally." We are, of course, free to disobey if we are determined enough, but the sense of inappropriateness is sufficiently strong that we rarely do. In a recent *Baby Blues* cartoon, a young girl complains to her mother that all the girls at her school dress the same, and asks: "Why can't anybody be different?" Her mother suggests, "You could be different." After a pensive pause, the girl, reaching out to embrace her mother for security, asks: "Why can't we all be different together?"[11]

To put the matter succinctly (and a little more technically), as we grow, we undergo the processes of socialization (being fitted to *behave* as expected within a particular social group) and enculturation (being drawn into a certain set of cultural *values and assumptions*). Before long, the patterns of behavior and meaning found in other cultures, patterns that would have become second nature had we grown up in those cultures, come to seem "weird" and "foreign," both of which are terms that implicitly declare that *we* are normal and *we* are the standard by which normality is to be judged. The day-to-day habits of our community help to sustain this sense of normality. At my local supermarket there is a section called "ethnic foods," where tacos dwell, but not hotdogs, as if hotdogs had no ethnic origin. When people I meet hear that I am not American, they do not say, "Your accent is different from mine!" Instead, they invariably exclaim: "You have an accent!" as if they had none. We operate out of a learned cocoon of cultural normality that may seem decidedly unnatural from across the border, or even across the street. This is our situation. How should we respond to it?

Gratitude

Both modern and postmodern mindsets grapple, in their different ways, with a Western ideal of the individual as an autonomous self, fully in charge of its own destiny, influenced by no one else, and able to sovereignly think its own thoughts. Modern perspectives have tended to embrace this ideal, while postmodern ones tend to emphasize the cracks in it. Both often imply that the influence of a particular cultural formation is primarily a form of disempowerment. Our particular cultural identity is seen either as something that we need to overcome to become truly rational, or as something that we will just have to put up with because there is no escape from social forces. Either way, culture seems to be standing in the way of our freedom. (Ironically, the person who protests loudest that she is not going to let anyone else influence how she thinks is in that very protest exhibiting the powerful influence of particular cultural ideals.) Within this sense of the world a kind of discomfort or discouragement can set in when we begin to realize how our cultural identities have been formed: if what I think and say and do is all just a cultural construct, then perhaps truth is a futile goal, faith is just an accident of birth, and beauty and morality are entirely in the eye of the beholder, at the whim of whatever a given group wants to affirm.

St. Augustine's reflections, quoted at the start of this chapter, offer a different point of departure. Augustine suggested that theologically, life begins with *gratitude* for graces received. Taking his cue, I suggest we should start with a basic thankfulness for the processes of formation that allowed us to be functioning persons at all. It simply does not follow that if we are deeply cultural creatures then all is reduced to preference, any more than the fact that we can only look at the world using human eyes (which are susceptible to flaws such as color blindness, and which perceive differently than, say, insect eyes) implies that we are not able to perceive a real world. Both truth and error come to us in culturally embodied ways (through words in particular languages, through books and images, through our interpreted experiences).[12] Similarly, if we had grown up outside any particular cultural formation, we would not have ended up free to be our true selves or infallible knowers of a culture-free truth. Instead, we would be very limited indeed. This is made clear by the rare cases of children who do in fact grow up outside human community, whether through abuse (such as being kept in isolated confinement) or early abandonment.[13] Such "feral" children, when they are discovered and returned to human society, commonly find enormous difficulty in learning a human language or interacting with other humans and exhibit animal-like behavior.

The famous experiences of Helen Keller provide a rare instance of an articulate report of former cultural deprivation. Keller suffered an illness at the age of 19 months that left her deaf and blind, severely limiting her ability to communicate with those around her. When she was six years old, her mother sought out a teacher for her, who was able to introduce her to language. Reflecting on the time before her teacher introduced her to the world of words, Keller later wrote:

> Before my teacher came to me, I did not know that I am. I lived in a world that was a no-world. I cannot hope to describe adequately that unconscious, yet conscious time of nothingness. I did not know that I knew aught, or that I lived or acted or desired. I had neither will nor intellect. I was carried along to objects and acts by a certain blind natural impetus. I had a mind which caused me to feel anger, satisfaction, desire. These two facts led those about me to suppose that I willed and thought. I can remember all this, not because I knew that it was so, but because I have tactual memory. It enables me to remember that I never contracted my forehead in the act of thinking. I never viewed anything beforehand or chose it. I also recall tactually the fact that never in a start of the body or a heart-beat did I feel that I loved or cared for anything. My inner life, then, was a blank without past, present, or future, without hope or anticipation, without wonder or joy or faith.[14]

Keller describes the time before she could use words to attach meanings to experiences as a time without the ability to distinguish precise feelings, without the ability to form complex interests in the things and people about her, and without the ability to think back or look ahead — a time of confused, inarticulate sensation.

To develop a more complex sense of self, we need language — and we cannot acquire language without acquiring a *particular* language.[15] The only way to learn to think is to acquire some particular concepts to think with. There is no way to learn "language in general," whatever that might be. The same goes for other aspects of cultural behavior. The only way to learn and expand our skills is to engage in the practices and use the tools found in particular cultural settings (whether footballs or fishing nets). The only way to learn to love others is to learn to love particular others and to express that love within a particular cluster of cultural expectations (where, for instance, buying flowers might be a better bet than offering a fish — or vice versa). And we seek and apprehend truth *with* the words, concepts, ways of learning, and instruments for examining the world developed in particular cultures. To doubt the existence of truth because of the unavoidable presence of culture is a little like doubting the existence of sound because of the necessity of ears.[16] Christian faith affirms that the most central revelation of grace and truth came when God became incarnate as a first-century Jew, and that the good news has been passed on to us through the Bible, a collection of writings from particular ancient cultures.[17] Grace and truth need not come to us disembodied, outside cultural time and space.

To be human means to be born *somewhere*, in a particular place and time, and to make connections with particular people. Strip away all the cultural particularities, all the influences of those who came before and alongside us, and we would not be left with a transcendent, universal self or with naked access to true reality, but rather with little more than bare sensation.[18] Realizing that we are cultural creatures does not throw out goodness, truth, and beauty — culture is the medium *in which* we become able to apprehend and respond to the good, the true, and the beautiful.[19] To receive an identity from a nurturing context that we did not construct is a kind of "primordial grace" — our culture is what God has used to gift us with our selves.[20] As Augustine recognized, the first response that we owe is one of gratitude for the immensity of what we have received.

REPENTANCE

Life is, however, not quite that simple, and the Western quest for autonomy reflects some legitimate anxieties. When it comes to culture, gratitude taken alone is problematic. The problem is that culture grows not from pristine demigods, but from the ways and choices of fallen people, and it is always a mixed bag of the good, the bad, and the ugly. The sin and alienation that are woven through our thoughts and deeds come to inhabit our cultures. Sin becomes apparent in culture in at least three interlocking ways.

First, our tendency towards pride, selfishness, lust, greed, anger, and various other vices seeps into the ways in which we shape our cultural lives together. When we give ourselves to the wrong things, that becomes reflected in our cultures. Perhaps we worship economic success — and foster among ourselves a set of cultural values in which ostentatious wealth is admired, poverty is despised, and environmental well-being is sacrificed. Perhaps chaste living seems too much of a challenge — so we tell one another stories in word and image in which spur-of-the-moment sexual promiscuity is normal, even liberating. Pretty soon it is significantly harder within the culture that we have shaped to be content with enough, or to be genuinely concerned with poverty, or to view others with chaste eyes. The cultural prompts that surround and inform us act as a continual undertow and make some behaviors easier and more plausible than others. In the worst cases — such as children born into wars or inherited drug dependencies — our very introduction to the world may be anything but nurturing. Any gifts received have been overlaid with wrong, with hurts, deceptions, failures, perhaps outright abuse. While all but the most catastrophically abusive upbringings contain elements for which to be thankful, it is also true that even the best of upbringings is not an unmitigated gift. Cultures as we experience them also contain poisons, and it's hard to feel fully grateful for a birthday cake that has razors in it.

Second, we all too often take the cultural identity that we have received and use it as a basis for looking down upon and judging certain others who do not share it. While thankfulness for the gift of life itself can be experienced by anyone anywhere, thankfulness for our cultural identity all too quickly becomes thankfulness that I have *this* identity and not *that* (inferior) one. Historically, fervent celebration of a particular cultural identity has tended to go hand in hand with various kinds of violence toward other cultural identities. We use cultural differences as weapons to secure our own superiority at the expense of others, and culture thus becomes a hook on which to hang our own pride, arrogance, insecurity, and anger. Messages of cultural inferiority are, moreover, often internalized by those on the receiving end, breeding feelings of hopelessness and lack of worth.[21]

Third, a further fruit of developing distorted cultural values and using cultural difference as grounds for judging others is the development of social structures and mechanisms that concretely disadvantage some. Attitudes begin to shape structures, with the result that some cultural varieties come to have more social power in a given setting than others. We differ culturally, but the differences are not all equal. As a British academic working in the American Midwest I find that my accent is an asset, because many people perceive it as "intelligent"; there are other accents, objectively speaking simply local variants in pronunciation just like mine, that might carry more negative connotations in the same setting, resulting in the speaker having to work harder to be taken seriously simply through accident of birth. Such small cultural differences become markers of cultural advantage or disadvantage.

Where the criteria for success become tied to the possession of cultural behaviors that are those of a particular group within society, inequality looms on the horizon. Think back to the discussion of Navajo rules of politeness in Chapter 2, according to which observing silence when spoken to is a mark of respect. Imagine (or, if this is your story, recall) the situation of a Navajo child in an Anglo-American school classroom. Research suggests that one of the foremost ways in which Anglo-American teachers make judgments about how "smart" a child is has to do with speed of verbal response.[22] The smart kids are those who have swift and ready answers to the teacher's questions. This expectation is reflected in our language — to call a learner "slow" is one way of suggesting lack of intelligence, and the opposite is to be "quick-witted." Students perceived as smart are, given human nature, more likely to receive the benefit of the doubt when their teacher is making borderline decisions about grades. If the teacher is not specifically sensitive to the cultural difference in communication patterns, there is a strong chance that it will be harder for the Navajo child to succeed than for his or her Anglo-American classmates.

Often exclusion develops into outright segregation or violence, where the disadvantage of belonging to one cultural group is made abundantly clear in denied access to employment or lack of personal safety. Even where such overt disadvantages are less evident, wherever one cultural group has most of the power to order how things work, culture works together with prejudice and power to make it harder in

subtle but concrete ways for those with other cultural identities to succeed. We make life harder for others, not because of any moral failing
or real deficiency on their part, but because we are able to enforce the
ways of doing things that make us most comfortable and fail to consider their effects on others. To the extent that this has become part of
the way things work, part of a structured system of behavior, it remains
an issue regardless of whether the individuals involved are personally
prejudiced — what is in the teacher's heart may do little to ameliorate
the way a particular school culture, for instance, operates.

Culture, then, is in several ways a mixture of the baleful and the
benevolent. Charles Marsh offers a striking example of the mixed
brews that we imbibe from our cultural contexts:

> In her 1943 memoir, *Killers of a Dream*, the Georgia writer and racial
> progressive Lillian Smith described her southern childhood as one
> woven of "dissonant strands" like "threads tangled into a terrifying
> mess." Sometimes "a design was left broken while another was
> completed with minute care"; quite often archaic and startling de-
> signs appeared in the weaving. The mother who taught her child all
> that she knew of kindness also instructed her in the rituals of keep-
> ing black people in their place. The father who chastised the child
> for her superior air toward her poor classmates also explained in
> careful detail that courtesy titles should never be given to black
> adults. "I do not remember how or when," Smith wrote, "but by the
> time I had learned that God is love, that Jesus is His Son and came
> to give us more abundant life, that all men are brothers with a com-
> mon Father, I also knew that I was better than a Negro, [and] that
> white southerners are a hospitable, courteous, tactful people who
> treat those of their own group with consideration and who as care-
> fully segregate from all the richness of life 'for their own good and
> welfare' thirteen million people whose skin is colored a little differ-
> ently from my own."[23]

This example focuses on particular sins of exclusion that were bound
up in a particular upbringing; the details of other experiences will vary
in many ways, but they will all share the reality that our cultures are imperfect, fallen, fractured, and less than or even opposed to the kingdom
of God on earth. The prophet Isaiah once cried out in the Jerusalem

temple, "Woe to me! I am ruined! For I am a man of unclean lips, and I live among a people of unclean lips" (Isaiah 6:5). We too find our own individual sinful inclinations augmented by our integration into fractured cultural beliefs, perceptions, and practices.

This does not cancel out gratitude — it remains true that my ability to write this sentence and your ability to read it, as well as our ability to engage together in moral reflection, depend on what we have received from many others. We did not make ourselves, and we have much for which gratitude is appropriate. Realizing the flaws, however, makes life much more complicated. We drink and are sustained, but the well is polluted, and the impurities take their toll. This caused Augustine to follow his meditations on the gracious gift of life with the exclamation, "Woe to you, torrent of human custom!" as he pondered the deformed nature of his own early learning experiences.[24] Gratitude is not enough. Repentance is also needed.

CULTURE AS CALLING

The complexity of our situation is bound up with human responsibility. Life is a gift, but it comes with a calling.[25] Unlike a rock or a tree, which are given an existence the nature of which is fairly fixed, human beings have been given real responsibility for shaping their lives on earth, and their basic beliefs and commitments play a role in how they shape their lives. At the beginning of the biblical narrative, we are presented with God's decision to make human beings "in our image, in our likeness," and to have them "rule over the fish in the sea and the birds in the sky, over the livestock and all the wild animals, and over all the creatures that move along the ground" (Genesis 1:26). Before long, the early chapters of Genesis show us humans being given responsibility for helping the nonhuman creation to thrive, and exercising creativity by naming the creatures around them (an activity that was God's in the early stages of the creation story). This responsibility to work with God in giving shape to an unfolding world is nowhere in these opening chapters of Scripture limited to some particular people group — it is assigned to humans simply as humans, male and female.[26] By referring to humans as made in God's image, the biblical creation story "suggests that humanity is dignified with a status and role vis-à-vis the nonhuman creation that is analogous to the status and role of kings in the ancient Near East vis-à-vis their subjects. . . . As *imago Dei,* then, humanity in Genesis 1 is called to be the representative and intermediary of God's power and blessing on earth."[27] We are called to imitate God in fashioning the unformed world into a habitable, harmonious home for all creatures.

As the early chapters of Genesis progress we see further examples of human creative responsibility as people build cities (4:17), design dwellings (4:20), make musical instruments (4:21), create metal tools (4:22), and engage in worship (4:3-4, 26). Notice that all this cultural activity, from naming to metalwork, affects the way people live together. If I name something, and the name sticks, then others will be constrained to use that name in conversation (Genesis 2:20 shows even God submitting himself to this limitation). If I design a city, others will live with the strengths and weaknesses of my design. If I create a musical instrument, its properties will influence the kinds of music that someone else can compose for it — and their compositions may in turn affect my tastes and experiences. Imaging God, and the resulting formation of culture, is not just about individual creativity. Small decisions and actions interweave into patterns of living over time, patterns into which others are born and which they must in turn perpetuate, reweave, contest, or unpick.

The huge problem is that by this time another element has entered the story — the boundaries set by God have been transgressed, and the fellowship between humans and God, among humans themselves, and between humans and the non-human creation has been disrupted, giving way to self-centeredness, alienation, and violence (Genesis 3). Along with cities, tents, wind instruments, and bronze tools come murder, polygamy, and vengeful boasting (Genesis 4:8, 23-24). The beings who create culture are gifted, called, fallen, fractured images of God, using their creativity to develop diverse cultural products, doing so in response to the same creation, and weaving their jealousies, falsehoods, and injustices into their developing cultures. And here am I, in the early twenty-first century, still having to contend with having been woven into a culture that is always a mixture of gift and fracture, truth and lies, nourishment and pollution, creation and sin. As an individual, I find myself a sinner in need of grace. As I come to understand how much of myself is embedded in a larger weave of cultural practices and assumptions, I find the same applies.

All of this suggests that some common responses to the realization that culture goes deeper than we often think are poor options. One response is a basic bigotry that loads all the good on one side of a cultural divide and all the effects of sin on the other. On the one hand, I might respond to questions of cultural identity by simply cheering for the home team and thinking of other cultures (if I think about them at all) as at best irrelevant, at worst weird or evil. The way that I live makes sense to me and my friends and family, and if others see differently, so much the worse for them — they are probably less developed or something. Although it often appears in the minor key of local small-mindedness, such cultural pride has been implicated in some of the worst violence perpetrated in history. It has found its most systematic expressions in the death camps of the Holocaust during the Second World War, as well as in more recent genocides. It may be less dramatic, but a similar despising of others is played out in ways with which we are sadly much more comfortable in every scornful glance directed at someone who does not share our color, clothing, tastes, or assumptions. Such an attitude both ignores the sin present in me and in my own culture and denies that members of other cultural groups may also image God. I may legitimately love my native culture, but I must do so without being blind to its faults, and without assuming that the call to image God is somehow uniquely reflected in my own cultural heritage.

On the other hand, perhaps in reaction to a painful awareness of bigotry of the first kind, I might be tempted to simply invert it: distant cultures are viewed romantically and lent a rosy glow, while my own culture is viewed primarily through guilty and cynical eyes. In this instance, I have learned to be only too aware of the shortcomings of the culture around me, am ashamed of its failures, and it is easier to project innocence onto other cultures that can function as a foil to my dissatisfactions with my own cultural home. Surely, however, the alternative to blind prejudice does not have to be an equally simplistic inverted prejudice that favors all that is foreign. Both options are overly hasty retreats from the complexity of the world. All cultures (including my own!) show some signs of having responded to a good creation, and are open to a redemption that does not simply obliterate them. As already noted, a retreat to cynicism may represent a failure of gratitude.

Firmly rejecting bigotry of any kind, others respond with a cheerful relativism that at first blush seems much more benign — we are all different, and none of us has the God's-eye-view, so let's just celebrate the differences and live and let live. There is a colorful carnival of cultures out there, and who am I to judge? While this has an element of appropriate humility, and may well be the right response to some aspects of culture (I love Thai food), it ignores the presence of sin. Because cultures are more than food, clothes, and dancing, because they embody our basic beliefs and values, our sense of who we are, what we should do, what we should hope for, and how we should relate to other people, cultures are not innocent. Cultures (including my own) and the practices they support may deny God, oppress women, erode community, legitimize various forms of violence, sacrifice children, or destroy the environment. Cultures also wield differing amounts of power over their neighbors at different times in history, and so are not simply different from one another, like colors on a palette; they are bound up with patterns of domination, exploitation, and exclusion (or of vulnerability, compassion, and embrace). A cheery relativism leaves too much unaddressed and ultimately shows insensitivity in the face of suffering, since it implies that everything should be left as it is.[28]

A third possible response is a passive fatalism that sees us as trapped in our particular cultural cages, unable to escape the forces that shape us. The conversation started before I got here, and there is nothing I can do about it, so I might as well shrug my shoulders and resign myself. This is a more pessimistic variant on the last option, and once again fails to take sin and suffering seriously because it fails to seek redemption. It ignores our continued responsibility to image God in the world. Cultures do, as we have seen, shape us in ways we hardly realize — but cultures also continually change as we continue to act. They are not monolithic entities, but are shot through with differences as different groups and individuals respond to their cultural resources in different ways. They are woven and rewoven from our day-to-day choices and moves. Recall that Lillian Smith, the Georgia writer describing the racism implicit in her southern Christian upbringing, became a proponent of racial equality despite that upbringing by embracing some elements of it and rejecting others. Culture is involved in all of our activities, and it gives us a set of biases, making certain responses more likely, but it does not determine what we do. We are responsible for its future.

Bigotry, relativism, and fatalism fail to take evil seriously — they all treat the cultural landscape as if nothing needs to be struggled against or repented of. For that very reason, they also all fail to demonstrate compassion for the victims of cultural evils. All cultures contain both gifts to be enjoyed and evils to be resisted. Scripture says "do not conform to the pattern of this world" (Romans 12:2); it does not advise us to simply lie back and accept as inevitable whatever patterns our cultures throw our way. Our cultures are fallen, but the offer of grace calls us to repentance, and repentance leads to renewal, to the New Testament's assurance that God sent his Son to "reconcile to himself all things, whether things on earth or things in heaven, by making peace through his blood shed on the cross" (Colossians 1:20).[29] To be Christian is to hope, trust, and participate in this work of renewal and reconciliation, and to seek, with God's help and continuing forgiveness, to order our own lives in its light. In terms of our cultural identities the Christian life involves a mixture of affirmation and resistance, celebration and mourning, gratitude and repentance. Complacency is not an option consistent with discipleship.

CHAPTER 4

ON LOVING FOREIGNERS

LUKE 10:25-37

On one occasion an expert in the law stood up to test Jesus. "Teacher," he asked, "what must I do to inherit eternal life?"

"What is written in the Law?" he replied. "How do you read it?"

He answered, "'Love the Lord your God with all your heart and with all your soul and with all your strength and with all your mind'; and, 'Love your neighbor as yourself.'"

"You have answered correctly." Jesus replied. "Do this and you will live."

But he wanted to justify himself, so he asked Jesus, "And who is my neighbor?"

In reply Jesus said: "A man was going from Jerusalem to Jericho, when he fell into the hands of robbers. They stripped him of his clothes, beat him, and went away leaving him half dead. A priest happened to be going down the same road, and when he saw the man, he passed by on the other side. So too, a Levite, when he came to the place and saw him, passed by on the other side.

"But a Samaritan, as he traveled, came where the man was; and when he saw him, he took pity on him. He went to him and bandaged his wounds, pouring on oil and wine. Then he put the man on his own donkey, brought him to an inn and took care of him. The next day he took out two denarii and gave them to the innkeeper. 'Look after him,' he said, and when I return, I will reimburse you for any extra expense you may have.'

> "Which of these three do you think was a neighbor to the man who fell into the hands of robbers?"
>
> The expert in the law replied, "The one who had mercy on him."
>
> Jesus told him: "Go and do likewise."

THE SCRIBE

The scribe was understandably upset. Setting out to put this Jesus character to the test, he had ended up on the wrong end of the debate, put in a false position by a clever story. And Jesus had managed to pull that off in such a way as to make it impossible for him to reply without humiliating himself. Worse still, Jesus had implied that he, a teacher of the law, was supposed to think of himself as on the outside seeking admittance to God's kingdom!

He had started the conversation by asking Jesus a theological question — what must someone do to secure a place among the people of God who would inherit eternal life? There was a standard answer, and when Jesus had thrown the question back to him he had given it: Love God with all your heart, mind, soul, and strength, and your neighbor as yourself. So far, so good. The next question was the crucial one. As a professional expert in Torah, the Law of God, he was confident of his own place in God's covenant community — but Jesus' actions and words had been suggesting a dangerous degree of inclusivity. Jesus had extended table fellowship to sinners, tax collectors, and prostitutes, and had even

---

On one occasion an expert in the law stood up to test Jesus. "Teacher," he asked, "what must I do to inherit eternal life?"

"What is written in the Law?" he replied. "How do you read it?"

He answered, "'Love the Lord your God with all your heart and with all your soul and with all your strength and with all your mind'; and, 'Love your neighbor as yourself.'"

"You have answered correctly." Jesus replied. "Do this and you will live."

LUKE 10:25-28

sent his disciples to the hated Samaritans — what did he mean to imply about membership in God's people? Hence the question. All present could agree that the Torah commands love of neighbor; that was not in dispute. But didn't it also say that the neighbor is my fellow Israelite, one committed with me to keeping Torah and avoiding defilement by sinners and foreigners? Here was a point at which to put Jesus to the test. Who was he saying should be treated as a neighbor?[1]

THE TERMS OF THE DEBATE

Jesus' parable about a compassionate Samaritan is one of those New Testament passages that has become almost too familiar, and has floated loose from its context. This makes it all too easy to hear it as a general moral exhortation to be kind to people in need. The idea of a "good Samaritan" (stripped of all its original shock value) has become a useful image to be applied to all kinds of attempts to do good deeds. Results of a simple library search for the term include government documents dealing with topics that range from the "Good Samaritan Food Donation Act" to the "Good Samaritan Volunteer Firefighter Assistance Act of 2003," and even the "Good Samaritan Abandoned or Inactive Mine Waste Remediation Act." Such applications are not totally misguided — Jesus would hardly condemn a general increase in compassionate acts. Generic uses of a vague "good Samaritan" motif do not, however, take seriously the situation in which Jesus' story is being told. What Luke presents us with is not simply the story of the robbed man and the Samaritan (the phrase "good Samaritan" does not actually appear in the text), but the story of how Jesus used this parable to unravel a scribe's mental world.[2] Pausing at this point to hear more carefully what this encounter has to tell us will help us to catch our bearings before moving on to look closer at some contours of intercultural learning.

The question that provokes the parable comes from a scribe, or teacher of the law, which is to say someone professionally engaged in copying the Hebrew Scriptures. Scribes were regarded as experts in

> But he wanted to justify himself, so he asked Jesus, "And who is my neighbor?"
>
> LUKE 10:29

scriptural interpretation, and it is no surprise that when one stands up to "put Jesus to the test" he does so by posing questions about how God's commandments should be interpreted. His questions are not, however, purely academic. Present-day politicians are put to the test in public by being asked carefully chosen questions designed to make them reveal their stances and allegiances on controversial topics. Something not unlike that is going on here. The scribe's opening question invokes Jewish expectations of a future inheritance, the "everlasting life" spoken of in Daniel's prophecies (Daniel 12:1-3). The point at issue was not so much individual salvation as the boundaries of the community that would together be saved because of their covenant with God.[3] It was the *people* of God who would inherit the kingdom of God; one question that had the potential to mark a person's position amid the religious and political debates of the time concerned who was in and who was out.[4]

> Do not seek revenge or bear a grudge against anyone among your people, but love your neighbor as yourself. I am the LORD.
>
> LEVITICUS 19:18

For the purists, the boundary was drawn in terms of ethnicity and obedience. Serious, covenant-keeping Jews were in; sinners and foreigners were out (compare Nehemiah 13:23-30, in which Nehemiah becomes violent in his attempts to purge Israel of anything foreign). Even the familiar command to love one's neighbor was interpreted in terms consistent with those boundaries. After all, Leviticus 19:18, the source of the command to "love your neighbor as yourself," explains the accepted meaning of "neighbor" — a fellow member of the covenant community, "one of your people."[5] The question of which specific others one should love was, moreover, a politically charged one in a land under Roman (i.e., pagan, foreign) occupation. The company Jesus kept and the things he said and did made him highly suspect in terms of boundary keeping. The scribe thought he should publicly check the small print, so he confronted Jesus with a follow-up question: What is your position on neighbors? Who are you saying is included in the people of God, the ones I should love?[6] Who is my neighbor?

THE ROAD TO JERICHO

Jesus responds, as on other occasions, with a story presenting the kind of extreme case in which matters easily papered over in everyday life leap into focus.[7] He evokes an Old Testament story about an episode of armed conflict between Judah and Israel that ended with folk from Samaria binding up the wounds of Judean war victims, applying healing balm, putting them on donkeys, and taking them home to Jericho (2 Chronicles 28:1-15).[8]

> So the soldiers gave up the prisoners and plunder in the presence of the officials and all the assembly. The men designated by name took the prisoners, and from the plunder they clothed all who were naked. They provided them with clothes and sandals, food and drink, and healing balm. All those who were weak they put on donkeys. So they took them back to their fellow Israelites at Jericho, the City of Palms, and returned to Samaria.
>
> 2 CHRONICLES 28:14-15

The setting that Jesus chooses for his own story is the road from Jerusalem to Jericho, a steep route through a wild region that was known as a dangerous spot for travelers. As soon as his story gets under way, its first curious feature becomes apparent: the main character (the only one who interacts with every other character) spends almost the entire story anonymous and incapacitated, perhaps even unconscious. (To get a sense of how noteworthy this is, imagine the story as a movie, with an A-list actor in the role of the victim.) This man, perhaps on his way home after visiting Jerusalem to worship at the temple, or perhaps just traveling on business, is attacked by robbers and wounded so badly that they leave him for dead.

This was not the way it was supposed to be. Journeys were always vulnerable times, open to the possibility of mishap, but being attacked, beaten, robbed, and left to die at the roadside is a profound wrong. If the man had indeed been to Jerusalem to worship, then cosmic insult was added to bodily injury. Could God not protect his worshipers? How could he allow this to happen? Was this man's sin greater than those of the others who passed that way? There was no indication that this was so. He was just, as the cliché has it, in the wrong place at the wrong time

— and having the wrong thing done to him, for the wrong motives. And so he lay bleeding, stripped, and motionless by the side of the road.

Perhaps the scribe allowed himself a wary smile as Jesus began his story. If this story was going where it seemed to be going then maybe Jesus' answer was going to be more conventional than he had expected. Be prepared to lend a helping hand to your brother in need who has fallen by the wayside. The Torah taught that if one were to pass another Israelite's donkey in difficulties, one should stop and help it (Exodus 23:5). How much more a neighbor, unable to get up from the roadside after an act of violence? There was little there that any God-fearing Jew could object to. On the other hand, one detail was troubling — Jesus did not actually mention whether the traveler was a Jew, and stripped and unconscious as he was, any passersby would have a hard time identifying which people he belonged to. Was the victim then really a neighbor who must be helped? Jesus wasn't telling.[9] There were signs that Jesus' hypothetical case was going to be more complex than it first seemed.

> In reply Jesus said: "A man was going from Jerusalem to Jericho, when he fell into the hands of robbers. They stripped him of his clothes, beat him, and went away leaving him half dead. A priest happened to be going down the same road, and when he saw the man, he passed by on the other side. So too, a Levite, when he came to the place and saw him, passed by on the other side."
>
> LUKE 10:30-32

Matters quickly got more difficult. A priest came along the road, one well acquainted with the requirements of the Torah, one whose life was committed to representing the people before God and returning God's blessing on the people.[10] God had not abandoned the victim after all — no sooner was he robbed than God's representative came along the road and saw his plight. Who better to help him? But Jesus had this priest walk right on by without even crossing the road. Perhaps he was concerned that touching a dead body would compromise his purity. Perhaps he had "important" business to attend to. Perhaps he was scared that the robbers still lay in wait for anyone who lingered too long. Or perhaps he was uncertain whether this bleeding victim was from the right group to count as a "neighbor," and felt that without such certainty the risk and inconvenience of helping were not required by the Law.[11] Whatever his motivation (Jesus leaves us guessing), he was soon gone around the next bend in the road.

Working through the common categories of Israelite traveler, Jesus announced the next character as another temple servant, a Levite. Another good, God-fearing, Torah-following (one might say church-going, Bible-believing) person. Another disappointment. Another hasty passage by on the other side of the road. Clearly, no help is to be hoped for from the temple servants.[12]

Perhaps the scribe now had a different idea of which way the wind was blowing. Jesus had long implied criticism of the Jerusalem temple hierarchy, telling people that their sins were forgiven without them having to go to the temple to offer sacrifices and receive forgiveness from a priest (e.g., Matthew 9:2-7). He sounded at times like another rural prophet from the north, speaking out against the southern seat of religious and political power. Maybe the next person along the road would be an everyday, salt-of-the-earth Israelite, perhaps a godly peasant who would show up the hypocrisy of the temple bureaucracy by demonstrating his commitment to Torah in a work of mercy.[13] That would work.

THE SAMARITAN

Jesus' actual next move could scarcely have been more offensive. The next person down the road was a Samaritan. That meant a good deal more than just someone from Samaria. The distinct history of the Samaritans went back to the defeat and exile of Israel when Assyria invaded in 722 B.C. As Israel was conquered, some of the people (including especially the upper classes) were taken off into exile, while many of the poor were left to farm the land, and were joined by and mingled with other displaced people, moved in as part of Assyria's empire management practices. The Samaritans claimed ancestry from the Jews left in the land, while the Jews regarded the Samaritans as at best mixed stock, their lineage compromised by the peoples relocated to northern Israel by its Assyrian conquerors (see 2 Kings 17:24-41). They also had the wrong religion — when the exiled Israelites did return to the land and began to rebuild the temple, the Samaritans opposed them (Ezra

4:17-23), and later built a rival temple in the north (cf. John 4:20). They shared with the Jews a commitment to the first five books of the Old Testament, but only those books — the rest they did not recognize as Scripture.

Jewish writings from the centuries immediately before Christ reflect animosity toward Samaritans; one text refers to them as a group that is not really a nation, but merely "those stupid people from Shechem."[14] In 128 B.C. John Hyrcanus, a Jewish leader, attacked Samaria and destroyed their temple; he later returned to besiege and destroy the city of Samaria itself. The Roman armies that occupied Israel in Jesus' day had in 63 B.C. taken Samaria from the Jews and returned it to the Samaritans. While Jesus was a child some Samaritans crept into the Jerusalem temple at night and scattered dead people's bones, desecrating the Jews' most sacred space and most central symbol. Some rabbis taught that accepting alms from Samaritans would delay the redemption of Israel, or that a Jew need not trouble himself to save a Samaritan's life. So Samaritans not only had the wrong ethnicity, the wrong faith, and the wrong politics; the Jews and the Samaritans had been engaged in a history of active hostility, up to and including bloodshed, for quite some time. The phrase "good Samaritan" has passed into the English language — but it is not a phrase that our scribe would have been likely to be caught uttering. Common Jewish attitudes in Jesus' day can be felt in the jibe hurled at Jesus on one occasion: "Aren't we right in saying that you are a Samaritan and demon-possessed?" (John 8:48). Jews despised Samaritans. If the question concerned who was in and who was out, Samaritans were most definitely out.

Jesus himself had recent experience that might have tempted anyone toward the same views. In Luke 9:52, just a little earlier in his journey toward Jerusalem, we are told that Jesus sent his disciples ahead to prepare for him to visit a Samaritan village. The Samaritans refused to welcome him. Jesus' disciples (who apparently did share the general sentiment) promptly offered to call fire down on them in judgment. Jesus, however, rebuked the disciples (Luke 9:55), and his tale to the scribe now echoed that rebuke. Not only did he have his Samaritan traveler show up the priest and the Levite by crossing the road and caring for the wounded traveler (who shows no indication of being a fellow Samaritan), but he rubbed the point home by dwelling at loving length on the details of the care he offered. The bulk of his narrative (over half) ends up being devoted to the binding and treatment of wounds by a *Samaritan;* the submission to personal risk, discomfort, and humility of a *Samaritan* as he lets the Jewish victim ride on his donkey, forcing him to walk like a hired servant and slow his journey; the decision by a *Samaritan* to stay overnight at the inn to make sure the victim got proper care (by no means guaranteed in the inns of the day);[15] and the payment by a *Samaritan* of all of the victim's costs to ensure continuing care until he was well.

> "But a Samaritan, as he traveled, came where the man was; and when he saw him, he took pity on him. He went to him and bandaged his wounds, pouring on oil and wine. Then he put the man on his own donkey, brought him to an inn and took care of him. The next day he took out two denarii and gave them to the innkeeper. 'Look after him,' he said, 'and when I return, I will reimburse you for any extra expense you may have.'"
>
> LUKE 10:33-35

And then came the subtly rephrased question. The scribe had asked who his neighbor was. Jesus refused to answer the question in the terms in which it was stated. Instead, he responded with a multiple-choice question in return. He offered a story with four characters, two Jewish, one of unknown identity, one a foreigner.[16] He then deftly excluded the one who might have been the scribe's first choice as the possible neighbor. He did so by the way he asked his own question: "Which of these three do you think was a neighbor to the man who fell into the hands of robbers?" With the victim in need taken out of the list, there are three choices left, and there is no way of choosing the priest or the Levite without appearing an utter fool (which was not likely to have been one of the scribe's aspirations). The scribe had to answer, but could not bring himself to say the "S"-word.[17] He answered: "The one who had mercy on him." The initial question has been turned on its head — it is no longer about classifying groups of people in terms of those who must be loved and those who need not be. It is now about the person who acts like a neighbor without raising questions of who is in and who is out, the one who has mercy, and this turns out to be a *Samaritan* of all people.

A Scribe under Pressure

By answering Jesus' newly framed question in the way that he does (and how else could he have answered?), the scribe must implicitly concede that Jesus is a better interpreter of the law. He must face the unwelcome suggestion that a person whom he most likely despised was a neighbor. He must also acknowledge Jesus' implied demand that he, like the Samaritan, should stop asking who his neighbor was in order to set up a neat list of exclusions, and instead set about *being* a neighbor, even across religious, ethnic, cultural, and political boundaries. Jesus may here be appealing to another part of the very text under debate, Leviticus 19. While verse 18 speaks of loving one's neighbor with members of Israel in view, a few verses later, in verses 33-34, the "love ____ as yourself" formula is repeated with a significant change. The command is now "Love *the foreigner* as yourself," and is reinforced by reference to Israel's founding experience of the Exodus, before which "you were foreigners in Egypt."

> Do not seek revenge or bear a grudge against anyone among your people, but love your neighbor as yourself. I am the LORD.
>
> When foreigners reside among you in your land, do not mistreat them. The foreigners residing among you must be treated as your native-born. Love them as yourself, for you were foreigners in Egypt. I am the LORD your God.
>
> LEVITICUS 19:18, 33-34

Jesus may (among other things) be insisting that these verses, echoing the call of Abram in Genesis 12 to be a blessing to the nations, form the proper context for interpreting verse 18. As Jesus said on another occasion, "If you greet only your brothers, what are you doing more than others? Do not even pagans do that?" (Matthew 5:47). Here in Luke 10 he intensifies the more inclusive thrust of Leviticus 19:33-34 in a pointed manner.[18] The bloodied victim is cared for by a stranger, and so, regardless of whether he was conscious of it, experiences a manifestation of the desires of God, a breath of the way things were supposed to be.

All this suggests that there is a good deal more going on than a gently moralistic injunction to be nice to people in need (which is, once again, not to say that if we were to do that on a regular basis it would not be a good thing). Jesus' Samaritan story does not let us settle for showing kindness to our compatriots and keeping our cultural boundaries intact. He offers the hated Samaritan (or the hated _____ [fill in the blank with whatever group of people you would not want your son or daughter to marry]) as an example of a neighbor — the Samaritan who helped another without asking about ethnicity.[19] As Darrell Bock puts it, "the lawyer's question about identifying his neighbor is really an attempt to say there is such a person as a 'non-neighbor.' Jesus refuses to turn people into a subspecies or into things that can be ignored."[20] Love your neighbor as yourself; by the way, your neighbor includes foreigners.[21]

I hope that by now it is becoming clear that Jesus' debate with the scribe has some bearing on our larger question of how Christians should approach cultural differences and intercultural learning. Questions remain, however. I want to further pursue two crucial ones in particular. First, what does learning about culture have to do with love? Second, doesn't thinking of cultural difference through the lens of kindness to a bleeding victim land us right back in the kind of condescension that was criticized in the prologue to this book, viewing the other peoples of the world as the needy objects of my glorious compassion?

THE LOVE COMMAND AND THE GOLDEN RULE

It needs to be emphasized, in case it is not obvious already, that in the context of Jesus' teaching, the idea that we should love those who are ethnically or culturally different has next to nothing to do with many of the meanings commonly given to the word "love" in current popular culture. The point at issue here has nothing to do with feeling romantic attraction toward foreigners, or thinking that all of their ways are so much cooler than our ways, or exclaiming with delight at their fascinating artifacts. "Love" in this context does *not* mean romance, attraction, or enthusiasm — our Samaritan was, after all, dealing with a dirty, bleeding near-corpse. It actually has very little to do with *liking*, in the sense of personal taste. "Love" here means "considerate responsiveness," a set of attitudes and actions that intentionally places the other's well-being at the heart of my concerns and responds accordingly.[22] We can see this from the way Jesus offers the Golden Rule as instruction in what it might mean to love one's neighbor.[23]

Compare the two passages from Matthew's Gospel found in the sidebar. Both the "Golden Rule" ("Do to others . . .") and the command to love one's neighbor are offered by Jesus as a summary of "the Law and the Prophets," that is, the Old Testament Scriptures. Partly for this reason, the two commands have been closely linked in Christian reflection on ethics since at least the turn of the second century A.D.[24] It has long been recognized (again since the early church) that the Golden Rule does not on its own provide a complete ethic or detailed moral guidance — taken on its own, out of its wider biblical context, it could, for instance, justify adultery.[25] The Golden Rule not only *sums up* the Law and the Prophets, but also *assumes* this larger biblical context, which, taken as a whole, implies that what should be desired from others and for others is that which leads to the joyful well-being that expresses the kingdom of God, and not the pursuit of self-centered ends. I am to seek the good of my neighbor within the context of the kinds of good that God's love seeks. As John Topel comments:

> "So in everything, do to others what you would have them do to you, for this sums up the Law and the Prophets."
>
> MATTHEW 7:12
>
> One of them, an expert in the law, tested him with this question: "Teacher, which is the greatest commandment in the Law?" Jesus replied: "'Love the Lord your God with all your heart and with all your soul and with all your mind.' This is the first and greatest commandment. And the second is like it: 'Love your neighbor as yourself.' All the Law and the Prophets hang on these two commandments."
>
> MATTHEW 22:35-40

> humans desire not merely material benefits, maintaining and ameliorating physical existence, but the whole range of actions which build a human community where the love of God is present and active, that is, the whole range of extraordinarily loving actions de-

scribed in the Sermon on the Plain. In short, the Golden Rule opens human moral obligation to the deepest human thirst for God's self-giving love toward his creatures, far beyond the kinds of actions that can be mandated by any natural or positive law.[26]

If these are our desires, desires not just for material benefits (though if we need such things as food, water, or clothing these are certainly included) but for the kind of treatment from others that expresses God's love, then we must confront Jesus' insistence that we love our neighbor by offering what we desire. Again, this may include material help, but there is nothing in the command to limit it to that; it may also include the offering of loving community, respect, considerate attentiveness.

Consider in the light of this the situation of the average English-speaking tourist. If I am that tourist, what does my typical behavior suggest that I want from others? I probably want them to invest the effort needed to be able to speak my language, so that I am not humiliated or inconvenienced. I am likely to want them to understand some things about my culture and my ways of behaving, so that they do not offend or misunderstand me. I may well want them to think well of me, to impute good motives to me and to my country, and not to make hasty negative judgments based on my nationality, language, or culture. I will derive pleasure from encounters in which people are attentive to me and willing to listen to my stories and questions. I want to be heard, valued, and respected.

"In *everything*," says Jesus (offering no wiggle-room whatsoever for saying that his words do not apply in this particular case), "do to others what you would have them do to you." (Perhaps we are tempted to ask: Which others? If so, we already have a Samaritan-shaped answer.) You want others to make life easier by learning your language? *Learn theirs.* You want others to understand you? *Work to understand them.* You want others to hear what you have to say? *Be attentive to them.* Right here Jesus articulates a central biblical rationale for taking the languages and cultures of others seriously and investing the sheer hard work necessary to attend to those who are culturally different and don't share my ways of speaking. Jesus also cuts to the heart of the ego-centric attitude (perhaps especially common among those of us who belong to more powerful cultures and speak more dominant languages) that assumes that the world revolves around *me* — that anything important will be said in *my* language, that the yardstick of normality and worth is *my* culture or ethnicity, that if any learning and humbling needs to take place it will be others who do it, and that *I* am the one who should be listened to most of all.

Note, in addition, that Jesus says nothing about waiting for others to do good to me first and then responding in kind. Quite the opposite: if our love is to reflect God's love, it has to extend even to enemies (Luke 6:32-35). We may desire a positive response from those to whom we extend care, but Jesus says we should not make our care conditional on that response occurring.[27] This goes far beyond what can be expected on the basis of what folk get away with in the everyday world of average human nature.

> "If you love those who love you, what credit is that to you? Even sinners love those who love them. And if you do good to those who are good to you, what credit is that to you? Even sinners do that. And if you lend to those from whom you expect repayment, what credit is that to you? Even sinners lend to sinners, expecting to be repaid in full. But love your enemies, do good to them, and lend to them without expecting to get anything back. Then your reward will be great, and you will be sons of the Most High, because he is kind to the ungrateful and wicked."
>
> LUKE 6:32-35

Jesus calls us to a much more radical love of our neighbor and, as we have seen, denies us the option of creating an ethnic shortlist of who counts as our neighbor. As we will now see, he also undercuts the option of thinking of ourselves as the noble helpers of the needy masses.

COMPASSION AND CONDESCENSION

Consider our poor scribe, confronted by Jesus with his tale of a compassionate Samaritan. The scribe asked a question to test Jesus regarding whom he was willing to include within the bounds of the people of God, and Jesus told him a story about hospitality toward strangers. I have suggested that Jesus' commands regarding love of others imply that we too need to become attentive and hospitable to those who are culturally, ethnically, or linguistically different. But here lurks a danger: that my familiar sense of the "good Samaritan" story will lure me (especially if I belong to a more powerful culture) into thinking of those outside my cultural group as inevitably poor, needy, and in need of my compassion (and of myself as nobly laying them across my trusty donkey). This leaves my own position in the driving seat intact, and can even allow me to feel good about my sense of superiority as long as I express it in hospitable acts of compassion. As Amy Oden notes, many of us would rather think of ourselves as hosts than as strangers:

> The feeling of pity and the desire to better the lives of others is a good thing, often inspired by God in one's heart. But it is seductive, even dangerous, for the host to view herself as the helper. The would-be act of hospitality becomes an act of condescension and failure to see, either one's own need or the true identity of the stranger as Christ. One can easily stay at arm's length and offer advice or solutions without actually entering the world of the other. Ego, self-satisfaction, a need to feel off the hook, demonstrating competence and righteousness, all too easily enter the equation, with the host as hero and the guest as victim.[28]

One last look at our Samaritan tale will point us in another direction. Consider again the way in which this tale speaks to its hearer, the scribe. When we read, watch, or hear stories we commonly get drawn into them by identifying in some way with one or more of the characters. Jesus told his story to a scribe who apparently trusted in his own place in the people of God and wanted to know who else he should think of treating as a neighbor alongside him. As this scribe listened to the story, with which of the characters might be have been able to identify as he listened?

The obvious possibilities can be passed over quite quickly. The characters in the story who are most like the scribe in their basic religious and cultural outlook are the priest and the Levite. It is possible that they are even asking themselves the scribe's question: is this victim really a neighbor whom I am obliged to help? But their conduct is so clearly placed under judgment by the way the story unfolds that for the scribe to identify himself with them becomes untenable. He can hardly applaud such callous behavior once the tale is told; if he did so, he would be speaking judgment on himself.

A second possibility is quickly made shocking by Jesus' narrative strategy. Most of us like to think of ourselves as basically good people. It is telling that tradition has turned the story into the parable of the "good" Samaritan — once the priest and the Levite have failed, we are primed and ready to identify with the good character, the one who comes along and resolves the crisis by doing the right thing. We are waiting to cheer for whoever does what by now we are waiting for someone to do. As modern readers, however, we have lost the sense of twisted gut that must have been experienced by the scribe when this anticipated hero turns out to be a foreigner, in fact a despised Samaritan, one with whom he would not normally eat, let alone identify himself. The possibility of imagining himself in the comforting noble role of the story's hero is destroyed — unless he is willing to first humble himself radically. The priest and the Levite are characters with whom he would want to identify, but cannot; the Samaritan is presented as one with whom he ought to identify, but he would hardly want to.

This leaves a last possibility. Formal analyses of the parable commonly point out that the wounded robbery victim is technically the central character in the story.[29] As already noted, he is the only one who appears throughout and who interacts with every other character. His innocent plight draws the hearer's sympathy toward him and rouses indignation on his behalf toward those who injured him or passed him by.[30] When Jesus returns the scribe's question about who is a neighbor, he significantly changes it so that it is put from the perspective of the victim. "Who is *my* neighbor?" becomes "Who was a neighbor *to the man attacked by robbers?*"[31] As John Nolland notes,

> When we are needy enough, neighbor help from anybody at all is very welcome. It is from down in the ditch that we need to contemplate the question of who our neighbor is. . . . From the perspective of the ditch it can only look mean and cruel to limit the scope of neighbor assistance.[32]

If the scribe identifies with the beaten man, then he must humble himself. He must admit his own need, see himself as lying lost and helpless, and step down from his pedestal in order to see the neighbor as one who may come to *him* with needed assistance. Foreign others are now no longer just objects of my charity — they are the neighbors that I need. Jesus describes the Samaritan as one who "had compassion." This phrase is used elsewhere in Luke only of Jesus himself (Luke 7:13) and of the father in the parable of the prodigal son (Luke 15:20). It is a characteristic commonly ascribed to God in the Old Testament. It is the love of God himself that is at work in this Samaritan. Like God, the Samaritan has compassion on a helpless victim who can only gratefully receive. Can the scribe imagine receiving compassion from a Samaritan, as from God?[33] (Can you imagine the grace of God coming to you through a member of an alien culture?)

As the conversation continues, the scribe's position becomes even more difficult. Jesus asks him which person acted as a neighbor, and he is forced to confess that it was "the one who had mercy." Then comes perhaps the hardest saying of all: "Go and do likewise." Remember that this started out as a debate about how to interpret the law, started by a scribe in order to test Jesus. The scribe's questions were a form of public challenge through which one aimed to win honor from the audience through providing a better account of the question debated than one's opponent.[34] Not only does Jesus make

> "Which of these three do you think was a neighbor to the man who fell into the hands of robbers?"
>
> The expert in the law replied, "The one who had mercy on him."
>
> Jesus told him: "Go and do likewise."
>
> LUKE 10:36-37

the scribe the one challenged and ask him to put himself in the position of the one needing help, not only does he represent that help as coming from a Samaritan and not from the representatives of the temple, not only does he embarrass the scribe's implied assumption that some are to be excluded from the command to love one's neighbor — on top of all that, Jesus now asks the scribe (of all people!) to *learn from a Samaritan how to interpret and obey the law.* This Samaritan understood the love command. Go and imitate him, learn your lesson from him. The scribe began by asking who else might count as his neighbor, as part of the true community of faith; he ends up receiving instruction (through a Samaritan!) on how he needs to change in order to be counted among the neighborly. Layer by layer, Jesus has mercilessly stripped away the scribe's ethnic and religious securities and superiorities. Mercilessly? Well, no. For the story does end with an invitation, an invitation to humble himself and enter the topsy-turvy world of compassion given and received in recognition of mutual vulnerability, and a life of loving God so wholeheartedly that cherished boundaries are redrawn.[35] The silence that follows Jesus' admonition may suggest that the price was too high for this scribe.

And what of us, Luke's readers? How will *we* place ourselves in the tale? If we know anything of Jesus' teaching it should be clear that any response that looks down from our own position of security — "Lord, I thank you that I am not like this scribe . . ." — will miss the point, and place us too under the judgment of Jesus' story. If we find ourselves among the culturally marginalized, ignored, suspected, or despised, then Jesus' call to "go and do likewise" should resound as a call to hope — in this tale Jesus raised up the *Samaritan*, the despised one, as the one in whom the love of God became manifest in the world.[36] Do likewise, show convicting compassion on the proud when their need becomes manifest. If we find ourselves among the privileged, members of a dominant language and culture, used to thinking of ourselves as the center and "foreigners" as oddities at the margins, then Jesus' call to "go and do likewise" has a different ring. Its undertones whisper: humble yourself. Realize your own need of mercy. Realize that God does not choose to live tamely within the circles of belonging that you draw. Learn from those who are of other cultures; God may be at work in *them* in ways that you desperately need. Hear the call to learn from the Samaritan, the stranger, who did not use a checklist of neighbors. Lay down your pride and seek to receive and offer a compassion that crosses cultural lines.

CHAPTER 5

PLAUSIBLE WAYS OF FALLING SHORT

Love your neighbor as yourself. Welcome strangers. Love your enemies. Do to others what you would have them do to you — in *everything*. Jesus called for radical love of those whose cultural identity is different — not a facile enthusiasm for the exotic, or a patronizing pity, but a genuine attentiveness that is willing to learn *from* as well as learn *about*. This strikes to the heart of our well-practiced egocentrism and ethnocentrism (the individual and group versions of selfishness). It should not be surprising if we find that in practice we have developed a creative range of ways of falling short without feeling bad.

Of course, the most obvious and direct way of failing to meet Jesus' challenge to intentionally love our neighbors is outright opposition, deciding to cling to our own prejudices and let our imagined world revolve around our own sense of security. We can simply reject what Jesus said as too hard or impractical and return to a familiar and comforting world of assumed cultural superiority. Some are even willing to go all the way and wear their prejudice as a badge of honor. I am assuming that readers who have made it this far have nobler intentions than that.

There are, however, more subtle ways of missing the point, ways that are more compatible with our desire to think of ourselves as good people (even good, *Christian* people). Alongside outright rebellion are various ways of simply falling short, missing the mark, perhaps shooting in the right general direction but failing to hit the target. This is what I want to address in this chapter: some thoughts and behaviors that have the appearance of heading in the right direction but do not quite arrive at the destination sketched in Chapter 4. I will look briefly in turn at concerns about staying true to my Christian identity if I really engage other cultures, at the temptation to see the ease of travel, the globalization of English, or the shrinking of horizons brought about by communication technologies as substitutes for genuine intercultural engagement, and at the idea that all of this is really most relevant to a few Christians who have particular callings as, say, missionaries or diplomats. After exploring these plausible ways of falling short, we will be better placed to take a closer look in the next chapter at what genuine intercultural learning will require.

Pleading Purity

Some Christian readers may have reached the end of Chapter 4 with a sense of unease. This is a normal reaction, to be sure, to paying close attention to Jesus' words, but the particular unease that I have in mind is the feeling that really opening up to learning *from* those of other cultures, as opposed to just safely learning *about* them, might in fact be a betrayal of one's Christian identity. The underlying train of thought might go something like this. I am Christian and also, say, American. My culture is in some sense a Christian culture, or at least has been strongly influenced by Christianity. Perhaps I identify strongly with a particular Christian denomination that has very definite cultural roots. Foreign cultures are more likely to reflect other faiths. If I really fling wide the doors of my heart and mind to learning from other cultures, then my faith is at risk, and I could be led astray. All this concern for intercultural learning must not be allowed to trump my faithfulness to Christian truth. And why should I give up being who I am anyway? Why should my cultural identity, within which there are accepted ways of being Christian, be sacrificed to someone else's?

It is true that faithfulness to the gospel takes precedence over the claims of worldly cultures where there is conflict between the two. It is true that one can be led astray by learning from another culture — as we saw in Chapter 3, cultures are not innocent; they embody our hopes and fears, our insights and our idolatries, and they have plenty of potential to lead us into evil. It is also true that the gospel places me under no obligation to abandon my cultural identity and copy someone else's instead.[1] These are legitimate and important concerns. A basic flaw in the train of thought just outlined, however, is the idea that the best way to be faithful to Christ is to listen *only* to the voices of my native culture — that my Christian identity and my cultural identity stand or fall together. This identifies Christ too closely with the ways of my community. Being Christian does not require me to abandon my cultural identity — redemption is for those of every nation, tribe, people, and tongue — but neither does it allow me to take my culture for granted as equivalent to the kingdom of God on earth.[2]

Assuming that the dangers are all "out there" in other people's cultures and the insights are all "in here" in my own culture will not work, either theologically or practically. Whatever role Christianity has played in the development of a given culture, that culture is neither purely Christian nor unfallen. I do not have to travel to find the danger of being led astray — I only need to turn on my TV, chat with my next-door neighbor, or read the newspaper. Since the particular temptations and distortions arising from different cultural patterns tend to vary, it may be that the ways of another culture bring a needed rebuke to my own familiar habits of mind and living. This does not imply swallowing whole any idea or practice that I find in another culture simply because it is exotic, or because it flatters my resentments toward aspects of my own community. It does, however, mean taking time to consider whether the voice of a cultural stranger can edge me closer to the contours of God's kingdom, enriching my cultural identity by helping to flavor it with love, compassion, and justice.

Some years ago I was told a story passed on from an Anglo-American teacher working with Native American children of elementary school age. Part of the way through the semester, the children complained that the teacher's way of grading was unfair. When I tell this story to the education students whom I teach, I often stop at this point and ask them to guess what was unfair about the grading. They usually suggest possibilities such as the grades being too low or too high, or certain children seeming to be given low grades because of their gender or appearance. Their suggestions tend to assume that an unfair grade means that some individual is not getting the credit they deserve for their own work — an unsurprising tendency in a highly individualistic culture where strong emphasis is placed on individual entitlement and competitive achievement. What these children complained about was different. How can it be fair, they wanted to know, if one or two children in the class are not doing well with the material, and you only give them bad grades, but give the rest of us good grades? Should we not all get bad grades because we failed to help them to learn and keep up with the rest of us? Why single them out as if we did not share any responsibility for the problem? The story raises uncomfortable questions for me as an educator. Which is closer to the ethos of the New Testament, with its talk of a body in which no part can boast and the weaker parts are given special honor — the competitive individualism that often characterizes Anglo-American classrooms, or the sense of communal responsibility evidenced by these Native American children? The answer to this question is far from simple, but the space for wrestling with it is opened up by hearing a question from outside my cultural world.

To discount such questions is to assume that I and those like me are more sinless and have more perfect wisdom than any other group on earth — an assumption that can only remain plausible if I keep myself locked in very small mental horizons. What theologians call God's common grace — the ways in which God sustains creation and human society and gives good gifts without favoritism — means that we may find truth in what seem to us surprising places.[3] In a famous passage concerning how Christians should read "secular writers," the Protestant Reformer John Calvin wrote that we should

> let that admirable light of truth shining in them teach us that the mind of man, though fallen and perverted from its wholeness, is nevertheless clothed and ornamented with God's excellent gifts. If we regard the Spirit of God as the sole fountain of truth, we shall neither reject the truth itself, nor despise where it shall appear, unless we wish to dishonor the Spirit of God.[4]

The same could be said regarding the "light of truth" that can be encountered in various cultures.

Moreover, the mental image of the world that places a Christian West over against a non-Christian rest of the world has rapidly become dated, despite its continuing popularity even in some academic conversations.[5] The greatest numbers of believers and the fastest rates of growth in the worldwide Christian church today are found in Africa,

Latin America, and Asia. At the same time, the church in many parts of the world is becoming increasingly ethnically and culturally diverse within particular locations, due to increased travel and migration. Philip Jenkins comments that "if we want to visualize a 'typical' contemporary Christian, we should think of a woman living in a village in Nigeria or in a Brazilian *favela*."[6] For Western Christians to close themselves to learning from cultural strangers, on the assumption that those people do not know God's ways (and Western Christians do), increasingly looks not only arrogant but ignorant. Whether it is the fruit of God's common grace at work among all people or of God's saving grace bringing into being a culturally, linguistically, and ethnically diverse Christian church, truth just as much as error can come to us from outside our familiar boundaries. If we risk dishonoring the Spirit of God by despising the truth arising from common grace because of its cultural location, how much more so when those from whom we could learn are brothers and sisters in Christ?

Of course, not every intercultural encounter will be revelatory. What about the times when the cultural others whom I encounter do not seem to be offering life-changing truths, but just different ways and ideas that are either hard to take seriously or easy to ignore? Here a basic truth applies that provides the most fundamental reason why tight defense of our own cultural purity is not an adequate response. Our identity is not separate from the way we treat others who are different. That treatment is part of our identity, for "as human beings we *are* the way we relate to others."[7] To be Christian *is* to love God with all my heart, mind, soul, and strength and to love my neighbor as myself. To have a Christian identity is to be a person who exercises such love. To think that I can protect my Christian identity by refusing the risks of love (the risks of learning love even from a Samaritan) is a contradiction in terms; it would be like trying to avoid health risks from food by deciding to never eat again.[8] The world is a place of darkness; it does contain falsehood and evil, and we will find their traces in all its corners — including our own lives and communities. The gospel of Christ calls us to respond not in fear and pharisaical judgment of others, but in critical attention to the planks in our own eyes, and in loving attentiveness to our neighbor (Matthew 5:43-44; 7:3-5).[9]

SETTLING FOR TOURISM

If a blanket fear of other cultures is too pessimistic, a second common tack is too optimistic. At the college where I teach, each student is required to gain credit for "cross-cultural engagement" before graduating. A few years ago, at the end of a presentation on the topic, a student approached me with a question. He and some friends, he told me, were planning to go skiing for a couple of weeks in Switzerland. Could they count this as their cross-cultural engagement experience, since they would be making their own way around in another country for a while? How would you have responded? Would you award credit for intercultural learning for a skiing trip to Switzerland? Think about the reasons you would give for your decision before reading further.

In 2006, the United States spent $72 billion on international tourism.[10] More people than ever before are traveling outside their own country. Does extended travel overseas add up to intercultural learning? Not necessarily. Overseas travel is of course a tremendous opportunity to engage in such learning. However, whether the opportunity results in significant gains depends on several factors.

On one of my first long journeys overseas, from England to Australia, I was interested to find that I would be changing planes in Bangkok, Thailand. I had never visited Asia before, and I had a vague mental image of Bangkok as an intriguing, exotic location. As I walked off the plane and into the airport, the first thing I noticed was a rack of Star Trek novels outside a bookstore — all in English and German. After some time spent wandering around the airport I had seen little that I had not seen at the airport I departed from — the same drinks, the same books, many of the same snacks. I could see little from the windows but concrete runways and parked jets. I boarded my next flight with a disappointed feeling of having traveled halfway around the world without actually going anywhere.

Obviously this was only the briefest of visits, and there was a whole country to explore outside the airport's peculiar cultural bubble. A few years later I had the opportunity to lead workshops for international English teachers in Thailand, and spent almost a week in Chiang Mai. I saw a little more than on my first visit, but only a little. The event was held at a resort outside the city. Resort staff spoke English, and Western food was served at mealtimes. One evening we were taken into town — and dropped off at an enormous shopping mall. After negotiating the local forms of public transport I was able to spend a couple of hours at a street bazaar, and that was as close as I got to really interacting with Thai culture. Even there the vendors were clearly well prepared to handle basic transactions with English-speaking tourists. There are a number of countries where I have stayed with and learned from local people and gained more of an inside sense of things; sadly, despite the excellent hospitality that I received, Thailand is still not one of them.

The point here is that there are ways of traveling that never really get outside the bubble. When visiting other parts of the world, it is quite possible (it happens every day) to travel around in a tour bus with others from your own culture, to spend your days interacting only with people who specialize in dealing with foreign tourists, and to spend your nights in hotels that are about as culturally varied as airports. In the process you'll show polite interest in some superficial cultural peculiarities, and come home with photos of beautiful scenery, odd road signs, and unusual buildings. To be sure, you may have had a memorable time, and your sense of the world will be somewhat bigger than if you'd never left home, but the amount of engagement with the people of another culture commonly remains minimal.

This can even be the case when the express purposes of the trip are educational or mission-related, if the visit is not designed to facilitate closer cultural engagement. Educational visits and mission trips can all too easily be little more than thinly disguised tourism. Studies of the effects of overseas study and mission trips on students' learning, maturity, and values have yielded mixed results, suggesting that participation in such trips is not in and of itself a guarantee of growth. In one study, involving students at Pennsylvania State University, it was found that when students studying abroad were fully integrated into the culture they were visiting (that is to say, staying among local people and participating with them in the daily rhythms of their lives), then those students experienced a significant increase in openness to diversity. However, when students stayed more isolated from the culture they were visiting, there was no change.[11] When visiting another culture as a group, strategies such as staying together in a hotel or hostel and traveling together in a bus risk achieving little more in character terms than strengthening relationships *within* the group as the shared travel experience brings group members closer together. This may generate little real engagement with members of the local culture, and may even intensify the sense that the locals are outsiders. If you have opportunities to travel abroad and really want to engage and learn, you need to take a critical look at how the trip is designed. If you are going to engage in guided study in a different cultural setting, it may be wise to ask your instructor exactly how intercultural engagement will be fostered and in what ways it will intentionally move beyond the starry-eyed romanticism of travel brochures.[12]

An incident during a visit to Germany with my own students came to symbolize for us the difference between tourism and cultural engagement.[13] It was 6:30 in the evening on New Year's Eve. We had landed in Germany earlier that day and traveled by train to Köln, where we were now braving the cold and the jetlag to wander across the Rhine for a New Year's Eve service. The massive Gothic cathedral, impressive enough by day despite the black cloak of mourning placed upon its shoulders by decades of air pollution, becomes almost unearthly after dark, a soaring, inscrutable thing lit against the night sky, countless tons of hand-carved stone somehow become ethereal. Earlier in the day tourists had milled around the interior, pointing at carvings, admiring the windows, gazing up at the impossibly high ceiling. Now perhaps a thousand worshipers packed the pews, with latecomers such as us still slipping in to claim standing room around the periphery. Two robed ushers stood courteous but vigilant guard at the barrier near the entrance, letting some pass, blocking the way of others.

The criterion for admission became clear as we approached the barrier. Just in front of me one of the ushers was calmly but insistently refusing to let a young man pass. Apparently the visitor did not speak German — the usher was repeating his refusal in several languages as the visitor made repeated gestures indicating his desire to enter. As we shuffled forward, the reason became visible: he was holding a video camera, and it was to this that the usher pointed as he persisted in his polyglot attempts to communicate that only *participants* were at this moment welcome: *"Missa, verstehen Sie? Missa, keine visitors"* ("Mass, you understand? Mass, no visitors," expressed in a mixture of Latin, German, and English). When our turn came, we passed the barrier with ease — a brief *"Wir wollen zur Messe"* ("We want to attend the Mass") was enough to be waved on into the church, leaving the frustrated tourist behind us.

It was easy to see why he would want to take pictures; the aesthetics were impressive, the sense of medieval drama vivid. The stained glass windows, spectacular by day, were now gray and lifeless against the night sky. But hundreds of candles, some of them on high ledges that left us wondering if the cathedral employed a stuntman to light them, flickered against the walls. Incense rose toward the distant ceiling from the altar, where a group of robed priests began the mass against the backdrop of swelling organ tones and soaring choir. Futile, of course, to think that any of this could be captured on film, but one could understand the impulse to try. The criteria for admission were, however, clearly and doggedly stated: worshipers only, no "visitors." Worshipers would need to get further than the aesthetics. They would need to attend to the liturgy, hear the sermon, participate in the offering; "visitors" were those who had merely come to stare.

Tzvetan Todorov describes the archetypal tourist as "a visitor in a hurry who prefers monuments to human beings" and who is concerned mainly with "the impressions that countries or human beings leave with [him or her], not the countries or the peoples themselves."[14] The tourist rarely engages in serious language-learning. Instead of facing the subtler and more arduous work of participating, listening, and beginning to weave human connections, the tourist is intent on capturing the moment on film to be digested later in the safety of the home, or shown off as a trophy to friends and relatives. The bubble within which such tourists operate is one that they take with them. As a result, tourists are often courteously but firmly shut out of the human heart of the culture they are visiting. They are left observing from behind a barrier. And all the time, the way through is not some arcane password, known only to the intelligentsia, but rather some basic ability to communicate and the simple desire to participate, to be included in some way in the Cardinal's opening cry, arms spread wide, of *"Brüder und Schwestern!"* ("Brothers and sisters!"), to be addressed by his sermon, to join in the prayers of the congregation. Engagement meant moving from "let me take your picture" to "let me stand alongside you and begin to learn"; from monuments to people, with all their hopes and concerns; from photos for later to participation now, being present, listening, and asking questions in the language of our hosts instead of gesticulating in frustration at an usher trying to tell us "no" in every language he knew.

To summarize, travel offers significant opportunities to engage with other cultures, but it is far, far from guaranteed that travel in and of itself will amount to much more than self-preoccupation in a more exotic location. Increased superficial exposure to members of other cultural groups may result in little more than solidifying existing stereotypes. This is not because tourism is in itself wrong — as a pastime, it can be rewarding and enriching. The question here, however, has to do with how intercultural learning can be a response to the call to love our neighbors. Tourism is often essentially about me and the quality of my experience (as evidenced by the average tourist's readiness to grumble when local customs, services, or facilities do not match their expectations); it is rarely about taking the time to learn from, attend to, and love the people whose space is being visited. Whether the destination is a distant country or a city mission a few blocks away, travel in itself is no guarantee of significant intercultural learning or neighborly love.

TRUSTING TECHNOLOGY

In the last hundred years the opportunities for interacting with people from other places and cultures have increased enormously, not only because of the possibilities for travel opened up by cars, ships, and planes, but also because of the rapid development of new technologies of communication. Where news of events in far-off places once took weeks or months to arrive, the world is now electronically delivered to our doorsteps with previously unimaginable speed and efficiency. It is not uncommon for my own morning at the office to begin with quick replies to emails written (sometimes only minutes earlier) by colleagues in Germany, England, the Ukraine, or Australia. I participate in meetings, some just down the corridor and some via teleconferencing with fellow journal editors who reside on the other side of the Atlantic. As I prepare to teach German classes, with a few clicks I can check the headlines in today's German newspapers and access video of current German news and cultural affairs. Advertisements, magazines, and radio and television programs vie with one another to bring me images of exotic locations and the people who inhabit them. One day recently I bought a German hip-hop CD from someone in Israel via an American auction site and paid for it in British pounds, all without leaving my chair in a city in the American Midwest — it was in my hands within a week. Increasingly, I can be in touch to one degree or another with folk from half a dozen cultures without traveling at all.

This massive increase in the availability of cultural data and contacts is easy to wed to a sense of technological optimism. Modern Western culture harbors a strong element of trust in technology to make things faster, easier, and better — to relieve us of the burdens of living. Speed and efficiency have become central values, and new gadgets are presented as keys to overcoming frustration. The continually evolving technologies of communication that connect us around the globe have both arisen from and helped to fuel the dream of instantaneous, frictionless communication with others. As John Durham Peters observes, "'Communication' is a registry of modern longings. The term evokes a utopia where nothing is misunderstood, hearts are open, and expression is uninhibited."[15]

It is commonplace for the imagery of contemporary advertising to connect this longing for complete removal of misunderstanding with the instantaneity and ease of technological gadgets. One advertisement for a telecommunications company promises to keep mobile phone users seamlessly connected in places like "Chilondoscow." Another asks: "Do you speak global?" A third depicts a finger on the button of a smart phone and instructs the reader: "To easily mobilize your global workforce, press here."[16] The underlying message of these modern-day parables is that communication technologies can remove the limitations of location and save us from misunderstanding; the competent user of technology will be able to transcend the frustrations of communicating across borders. Similar messages accompany technologies promising unprecedented ease of learning new languages. We are constantly being sold the idea that the right technology will bring down intercultural barriers, connect us all clearly and cleanly with one another, and get rid of the tedious necessity of laboring to listen and to understand.

If only it were that easy. The reasons why it isn't can be illustrated from recent studies of a set of email exchanges that occurred as part of language classes for some undergraduate students. English-speaking North American students in their fourth semester of learning German were paired up with German students studying to become teachers of English in Germany. The two groups of students studied the same books and movies and were expected to engage in email conversations about them using both English and German. These exchanges were intended to offer opportunities to correct one another's language and to learn about one another's cultural perspectives. One might expect email to help cultural differences to fade into the background. There is no body language to interpret; no unusual appearance or clothing to react to; no visible age, gender, or ethnicity; no awkward negotiation of silences between utterances. Instead there are just words typed and read on keyboards and screens that vary little the world over, communication technology bringing the world closer together.

Julie Belz has analyzed in detail the difficulties that arose in a number of the exchanges between particular German and American students.[17] In one exchange, between Eric in the United States and Anke and Catharina in Germany, Eric ended up withdrawing in anger partway through the semester and refusing to engage in further email communication. Study of transcripts of the email conversations shows misunderstandings on both sides caused by differences in German and American communication styles.[18]

When Eric writes to his German partners we find him, not surprisingly, using communication patterns broadly typical of English-speaking European Americans. When called upon to critique the ideas or language of Anke and Catharina he avoids open confrontation, makes sure that any negative comments are qualified and preceded by plenty of positive praise, and works to sustain a gracious, accommodating tone. His words focus more on social bonding than information:

> I am glad you liked our home page, I spent a lot of time working on it! Your english is very impressive. My german is not nearly that good so you're probably gonna have a lot of errors to correct. I actually had a hard time finding many errors in your e-mail. I guess I will begin by correcting a few of your english errors.[19]

When his partners ask pointed and controversial questions he sidesteps them, avoiding certain topics altogether in his replies and appealing to the need to concentrate on topics prescribed by the instructor as a way of keeping the conversation within certain bounds without having to express direct personal resistance. When discussion of the books and films leads him to raise questions that could be controversial or offensive to the German students, he finds ways of distancing himself from the question (such as ascribing it to his instructor) and of leaving plenty of space for Anke and Catharina to disagree:

> I would like to reply to all the questions you've asked in your e-mails, but first I have to write about the stuff that we are reqquired to talk about.
> Meine Lehrerin meint dass "Disney hat das deutsche Kulturgut gestohlen. . . ." Was meinst du ueber diese Idee?" [My teacher thinks that Disney stole German cultural heritage. . . . What do you think about this idea?][20]

Anke and Catharina, again unsurprisingly, stay closer to communication styles commonly followed by native German speakers. They are more concerned with stating the facts and discussing information than with being deferential, and make more categorical statements than Eric does. When they have criticisms they state them directly and up front, and use different strategies to soften them (such as assurance that "I'm sure that you must have known this already," which could sound like an added criticism to Anglo-American ears). They ask direct questions about controversial topics, they are happy to disagree openly as a mark of frank and serious discussion, and they accordingly react negatively to perceived avoidance of the issues; commitment to debating the truth of the information under discussion takes precedence over deferential moves:

> Anyway we did wrote you one letter in German, one in English that we both didn't like any of the two movies. They were boring and they were full of drug abuse. I can't take anyone serious who is a pot smoker or an alcoholic. Well they spoke about sexuality and life and so one but in such a boring way . . .
>
> By the way, we think it is sad that you only write to us about the thinks the teachers tells you to. . . . Don't you have the time to write us anything personal?[21]

On each side of the exchange the students' familiar cultural styles of communication unconsciously shape the ways in which they write and how they interpret the messages that they receive. Such styles are learned early in life and are hard to change. To Eric, the more direct style of the German students apparently came across as overly harsh, critical, aggressive, and overbearing. To a German eye, Eric's more deferential style can easily position him as a conversation partner who is superficial and uninformed, unwilling to commit himself or stand up for a viewpoint, too eager to hide behind others' opinions, and shallow and boring because of his tendency to shy away from disagreement and his apparent lack of interest in his conversation partners' real opinions. There is plenty of fuel here for misunderstandings, and the lack of body language, tone of voice, and immediate feedback that characterize email communication may actually make matters worse, making it harder to pick up the emotional tone of a message accurately. On both sides, knowing more about both styles of communication might have helped lead to a more positive outcome.

This is, of course, more of what we have seen in earlier chapters — our cultural identities shape the ways in which we find it natural to interact and make us feel that our own ways are normal. The point here is that the shift to email as the medium of conversation did not remove these intercultural dynamics; it simply provided a new stage for the same drama to be enacted.[22] It is true that technologies of communication can bring us into new kinds of proximity — before the Internet,

Eric and Catharina and Anke may never have interacted at all. This gives us new kinds of opportunities for intercultural learning. The dream that these technologies will simply remove all the effort and make us all understand one another remains, however, a dream. Gluing a phone to our ear or our eyes to a screen does not pry us loose from our cultural settings and identities. Technology is an important part of the bigger picture, but it leaves firmly in place the challenge of learning to hear cultural others and interact with them lovingly.

RELYING ON ENGLISH

A further temptation applies most strongly at the present time to native speakers of English, though others are not immune to similar impulses. Nicholas Ostler comments in his sweeping survey of the careers of the world's languages that "the glories of any language community are hard for a speaker-patriot to resist, and few have any true conception of ages other than their own."[23] To "ages" he could well have added "places" and "speech communities." As we saw in Chapter 3, our instinctive preference for our own mother tongue (or tongues) begins to be formed even before birth; before very many years have passed we reach a stage of development where adding mastery of further languages requires considerable effort. Our naïve experience of the world tends to subtly confirm our prejudices. Our own language seems easier to pronounce than others, and of course for us, who have been practicing since birth, it is. Our own language seems to express meanings in ways that make good sense of the world, especially when compared to the seemingly odd and awkward concepts that we find in other languages, and of course for us, who have been learning to think this way for longer than we can remember, it does ring true. Naïve and suspiciously self-serving as the exercise may be, there has been no shortage throughout history of people willing to declare their own language (whichever language that happens to be) to be the most elegant, the most beautiful, the most practical, in general the most excellent language on earth.

The temptation has been particularly strong for those who happen to grow up speaking a language that has gained significant power, influence, and geographical reach at the time in which they live. Lan-

guages, like cultures, wax and wane in power and prestige. For as long
as there have been people with different languages trading with, negotiating with, and warring with one another, there has been a tendency
for one or another of the languages of the day to serve as a *lingua
franca* — a shared bridging language used in addition to individuals'
mother tongues to get certain things done (from doing deals to running empires). Some such languages of convenience remain quite local; others, such as Sanskrit, Aramaic, Arabic, Greek, Latin, French,
Spanish, and Russian, have at different times spanned large sections of
the world. It is tempting (especially for its native speakers) to ascribe
the success of the currently dominant language to its positive qualities
as a language. In fact, such arguments hold little water linguistically or
historically. As linguist David Crystal observes:

> A language does not become a global language because of its in-
> trinsic structural properties, or because of the size of its vocabulary,
> or because it has been the vehicle of a great literature in the past, or
> because it was once associated with a great culture or religion. . . . A
> language has traditionally become an international language for
> one chief reason: the power of its people — especially their political
> and military power. . . . The history of a global language can be
> traced through the successful expeditions of its soldier/sailor
> speakers.[24]

Due to a series of historical developments centered around the
military and political power of Great Britain during the time of the British Empire and more recently the economic, military, and technological might of the United States of America, English has come to function
as a global language. As a result, it is possible in many parts of the world
to carry out certain activities in English — traveling, finding food and
accommodation, and conducting certain business transactions, academic discussions, and political negotiations. Like tourist package
deals and computer software, global English beckons us to see it as a
handy shortcut that will save us the labor of intercultural engagement.
Like travel and technology, it can certainly help, but it will not get the
job done, for several reasons.

First, as we have already seen, speaking the same language is no
guarantee that cultural meanings are being shared. Recall, for instance,

the story in Chapter 2 about Navajo patterns of silence in conversation. Such differences are common. One study examined the conversation patterns of female French and North American guests at dinner parties, looking in particular at the patterns of turn-taking in the conversation. The North Americans tended to maintain brief pauses between conversational turns, whereas the French tended to overlap their utterance with that of the previous speaker. In interviews conducted after the parties, the North Americans reported perceiving the French as interrupting them rudely, while the French saw the North Americans as slow and boring conversationalists.[25] Such effects do not disappear simply because both parties are using English.

Moreover, as English continues to evolve around the world, it is far from guaranteed that speakers of different varieties will mean the same things by the same phrases. I have heard virtually identical stories from two female North Americans about incidents while visiting England and staying with British families. In each case the father in the host family concluded the evening's conversation by inquiring of his guest (to her considerable horror), "Would you like me to knock you up in the morning?" In British English the phrase "to knock up" means no more than to knock on someone's door to make sure they are awake in time for the day's schedule — it has nothing to do with the idea of being made pregnant that it evoked in the minds of the North American guests. Again, the need for some cultural understanding does not evaporate simply because everyone present is speaking English.

Second, the notion that English works everywhere is a considerable exaggeration. As Crystal notes on the basis of a compilation of recent statistics regarding the global number of users of English:

> If one quarter of the world's population are able to use English, then three quarters are not. Nor do we have to travel very far into the hinterland of a country — away from the tourist spots, airports, hotels, and restaurants — to encounter this reality. Populist claims about the universal spread of English thus need to be kept firmly in perspective.[26]

As Crystal's comment highlights, while English is very widespread, there are upward of four and half billion people who do not speak or understand English. Even in a medium such as the Internet, dominated by English in its early years, the share of the World Wide Web that consists of web pages in English is shrinking as a proportion of the whole as new regions come online. By the early 2000s, non-English-speaking users of the Internet outnumbered English-speaking users, and the composition of the Internet continues to change rapidly. Quoting figures obtained in 1996, Crystal reported that at that point an Internet search for the German word *Orchester* (orchestra) produced a total of 76 hits (of which 34 pointed to pages in English).[27] The same search carried out using the search engine Google on December 3, 2007, yields 790,000 total hits for *Orchester;* however, the same search conducted using www.google.de, Google's German portal, yields 6,770,000 hits, and restricting the search on the same site to pages in German yields 1,960,000 hits. Clearly, using an English-based search engine severely curtails one's impression of what exists on the Internet, even if one is actively searching for non-English terms.

Moreover, and perhaps more important in the present context, relying on English can in many cases restrict our interactions to certain largely tourist-oriented locations and to those segments of the population who are either trained to serve tourists or who are highly educated and affluent, for these are the people most likely to have learned English.[28] This ought to make Christians in particular pause for reflection. Jesus was hardly renowned for hanging out only with the wealthy and well educated. Theologian Lesslie Newbigin puts his finger on the problem in the course of arguing that Western Christians badly need to listen to and learn from the witness of Christians in other cultures:

> The difficulty is that most of us are not able to listen to them until they can speak to us in our language. Only those who have been co-opted into our culture by receiving what we call a modern scientific education are able to join in dialogue with us. The others, however charming they may be, however profitable to the tourist industry, are not potential partners in dialogue.[29]

By relying on English alone, native speakers of English risk restricting their interactions to those members of another culture who are most cosmopolitan and most like themselves. They risk remaining unable to listen to those who are not part of the elite and projecting an image of indifference or even disrespect to those outside the English-speaking network. In so doing, they identify themselves in many settings squarely with power and privilege.[30] Each of these matters, all at least partially remediable by some effort given to language-learning, should perturb those who wish to follow Jesus closely.

Third, it is painful but necessary for English speakers to realize that even in cases where it is possible to get things done in English, the undertones implicit in doing so may be far from positive. In some parts of the world, English comes with a bad taste for historical reasons. As already noted, the spread of English has historical connections with the spread of empire, connections that have been quite explicit and intentional. One British writer wrote in 1801:

> If many schools were established in different parts of Asia and Africa to instruct the natives, free of all expense, with various premiums [prizes] of British manufacture to the most meritorious pupils, this would be the best preparatory step that Englishmen could adopt for the general admission of their commerce, their opinions, their religion. This would tend to conquer the heart and its affections; which is a far more effectual conquest than that obtained by swords and cannons: and a thousand pounds expended for tutors, books, and premiums would do more to subdue a nation of savages than forty thousand expended for artillerymen, bullets, and gunpowder.[31]

The notion of English as a tool to "subdue . . . savages" was hardly calculated to leave only sweetness and gratitude in its wake. In some places there are memories of children being beaten if they spoke in their mother tongue instead of in English anywhere near the school building, or of children being renamed with English names in order to (in the words of one British colonial governor) release them "from a state of barbarous insignificance." In India, Mahatma Gandhi referred to the imposition of English as a sign of slavery.[32] As Crystal comments:

> People have a natural wish to use their own mother tongue, to see it survive and grow, and they do not take kindly when the language of another culture is imposed upon them. Despite the acknowledged values which the language of that culture can bring, English has an unhappy colonial resonance in the minds of many, and a history where local languages could easily be treated with contempt.[33]

Such responses are, moreover, not restricted to older British colonial history. The position, actions, and cultural exports of the United States on the world stage have their own potential to lead to associations of English with coercive power and cultural imperialism in the minds of some speakers of other languages. Negative perceptions may be encountered not only in the places where there are obvious reasons for resentment. One discussion of the global place of English cites the comments of a Japanese journalist from the mid-1990s: "Americans take it for granted that foreigners should speak English. That is linguistic imperialism and Americans should give up that idea. I believe Americans respect fairness, but as far as language is concerned, they are not fair. For example, the U.S. Ambassador has never held a press conference in Japanese."[34] Reaching out to another in his or her own language is often warmly received as a sign of respect. It is equally the case that the opposite, a lack of evidence that any effort to do so has been made, can easily be interpreted as a lack of respect. Oblivious or willful indifference to such sensitivities is only likely to make matters worse.[35] Whether we believe such perceptions to be justified or not, the reality is that while there are places in the world where English is welcomed, there are also places where English carries at best very mixed connotations. Again, this should perturb those who wish to respond to Jesus' call to do to others as we would have them do to us.

In the end, as we saw in Chapter 4, it is the Golden Rule that most succinctly challenges a utilitarian over-reliance on English as the medium for interacting across cultures. In everything, do to others as you would have them do to you. Our preference when it comes to others' behavior towards us is overwhelmingly for being heard and addressed in our own language(s), in which we are able to be at our most comfortable and most persuasive.[36] Clearly it is not possible to learn all of the world's languages, but that will hardly do as an excuse for making no effort to learn any. It is not possible to learn all of the world's cultures either — the important question is how exactly we will interact with those cultures (and languages) with which our location, our opportunities, and our callings lead us to seriously engage. It is perhaps partly because language learning takes serious time and effort, and even a little humiliation, that even a halting and imperfect effort to speak to another in his or her own language is so often received as a token of good will. To speak or listen to someone in their own language communicates that they are important enough for me to invest time and effort in learning the way they speak and hear. This is perhaps especially so if I am a native speaker of English, since it goes against the stereotypical image of the monolingual English speaker, indifferent to the languages of others, thus providing a welcome surprise. In the world as we find it, there will inevitably be many occasions where the most practical way of communicating is to use English as a bridge. There will, however, also be many settings where this is not the ideal solution. If the aim is to love my neighbor as myself, then the most basic question is not what works pragmatically, or what is the least I can get away with, but rather what best honors the others with whom I am engaging. Such honoring does not come for free.

LEAVING IT TO THE SPECIALISTS

Finally, another all-too-plausible roadblock on the path to full investment in intercultural learning is the assumption that such learning is really the need of a specialized few with peculiar callings — it does not really apply to me because I am not called to be a diplomat, relief worker, or so forth. To be sure, folk in those specialized callings will need skills in dealing with cultural difference, but such skills are less relevant to the rest of us. Put in more religious terms, surely this is a matter for career missionaries, for those who will live and work for extended periods overseas. If my calling is not to preach the gospel abroad then my need for intercultural learning ought to be minimal. Many Christian books on cross-cultural learning serve to reinforce this impression. Why foist on everyone a kind of training that is really for the career experts?

As I indicated in the Prologue, part of the underlying purpose of this book is to resist this assumption that the reasons for Christians to engage with intercultural learning are restricted to the missionary call (or its secular analogies). Even if we accept the idea that the reasons for intercultural learning must be career-focused (I will question this presently), the idea that this makes it the preserve of a select few is decreasingly viable. It is not possible within the scope of this book to embark on an exhaustive survey of the ways in which the need to be able to handle cultural difference with sensitivity arises in different careers. A few examples will, however, suffice to show that the net must be cast much more broadly than diplomats and missionaries.

Business

A pair of researchers taped and studied business meetings held between British and Chinese company officials. These meetings were hosted by the British company with the specific aim of welcoming their Chinese customers and building good business relationships. While the British hosts felt that the meetings had gone well, the researchers' study of the conversations and interviews with the Chinese delegates told a more complex tale. Here is how one meeting started:

> Shortly after the British chairman had welcomed the visitors, he asked the British staff to introduce themselves. When they had done this, he invited each of the Chinese visitors to introduce themselves. This immediately caused confusion among the visitors. The delegation leader turned to consult the others, and one of them requested in Chinese that he do it on their behalf. The leader then started to speak on behalf of everyone, but the interpreter interrupted him saying, in Chinese, that they should first introduce themselves. This resulted in further worried faces and discussion in Chinese, and it was nearly a minute before the visitors started introducing themselves individually.[37]

It was clear from the follow-up interviews that the British participants were puzzled at the delay, and put it down to problems with language. The Chinese, however, explained that for the delegation leader to speak on everyone's behalf "is the normal way." They had trouble adjusting to what was for them a foreign practice of each person introducing himself or herself in turn.

As the meeting drew to a close another difficulty arose, again undetected by the British hosts. The British chairman explained the arrangements that had been made for the Chinese guests and then brought the meeting to a close, feeling that the conversation had been informal and cordial and reflected good progress in the relationship. The Chinese, on the other hand, were offended that they had not been given a chance to make a speech in return before the meeting finished. The delegation leader later explained:

> According to our home customs and protocol, speech is delivered on the basis of reciprocity. He has made his speech and I am expected to say something. . . . Condescension was implied. In fact I was reluctant to speak, and I had nothing to say. But I had to, to say a few words. Right for the occasion, right? But he had finished his speech, and he didn't give me the opportunity, and they each introduced themselves, wasn't this clearly implied that they do look down upon us Chinese.[38]

Such examples are far from isolated. Not only in sales, but in an array of areas ranging from hiring to performance evaluation to management to advertising to simply honoring one's coworkers on a daily basis, cultural sensitivity has become an important skill for anyone who desires to live out love for their neighbor in the business world.

Housing

In an article exploring how our basic visions of life shape the ways in which we design our living spaces, Brian Walsh relates the story of attempts to forcibly assimilate the Anishinaabe people of Grassy Narrows in Ontario, Canada, to the ways of the mainstream Canadian culture.[39] The story begins with the relocation of these aboriginal people from their traditional homes to suburban-style government housing in the name of development. As Walsh summarizes the motives of the government agencies involved, "Surely access to better roads, health care, an on-site school, electricity, wage-paying jobs, more efficient infrastructures, and higher standard housing would make life better for the Grassy Narrows people."[40] In fact the change in housing proved deeply demoralizing for several reasons related to basic cultural values.

Walsh explains that in the traditional settlement, people lived spaced apart, with particular spaces assigned to particular clans and high value placed on respect for others' space.[41] In the new housing development, houses were crowded together and were not allocated in ways that would preserve clan identities, copying the dominant culture's pattern of random distribution of individual family units in tightly clustered housing. Moreover, the old settlement was constructed as a series of circular compounds. This gave all equal access to running water, which was important both for livelihood and because of beliefs about the importance of being near living water. It also reflected a basic cultural motif of the circle representing community, wholeness, and well-being. The new settlement was designed (again in a way familiar to mainstream city planners) in a series of linear blocks by a stagnant lake. All of these changes created a new living space in which it was extremely difficult for the Anishinaabe people to sustain respect in the ways they were used to, to maintain community structures, and to feel at home in the world. The new settlement, regardless of its quality in terms of the dominant community's standards of government housing design, contributed to the erosion of community values and well-being. As one elder explained, "On the old reserve, you knew your place. . . . As soon as they started to bunch us up, the problems started, the drinking, the violence."[42]

As Walsh indicates in his article, this is not an isolated instance, but part of a wider pattern of problems arising when housing is designed for and assigned to groups of people without careful consideration of their cultural identities and ways of interacting. Working to provide housing without cultural sensitivity may do little to provide a sense of home, and once again a desire to serve may end up doing harm.

Health Care

It is by now widely accepted that health care involves far more than the provision of medications, and that cultural sensitivity is an essential component of a doctor's or nurse's competence. Issues as varied as differing perceptions of time (which affect patients' attitudes to appointments and treatments), differing understandings of health and of symptoms, different attitudes toward the medical profession, lifestyle differences, questions of who should have say over the treatment of a child (the parents? the wider family group? the community elders?), and interpretations of a nurse's or doctor's actions affect the quality of health care provided, and have led to the growth of courses in cross-cultural nursing. Where cultural awareness is not present, misunderstandings can easily lead to distress for patients.

Paja Lee Donnelly describes the case of Mrs. Hwa, a 65-year-old Korean woman who went to a hospital with severe abdominal pain during a visit to the United States. She did not speak English. Donnelly relates:

> When repeated blood samples had to be taken, the patient became frightened and began to scream. The staff nurse tried to hold her down while the blood was being withdrawn, but that only intensified her agitation. After that, the patient did not want the nurse to come near her and continued to yell. A psychiatric consultation was ordered, which resulted in Mrs. Hwa being medicated with Haldol, a powerful psychotropic drug. The following morning, when her daughter came to visit her, she was stunned to see her mother's condition. The drug had produced serious side effects, causing slurred speech and a rigidity of the hands. The daughter immediately arranged for her mother to be discharged from the hospital because of the treatment inflicted upon her.[43]

In this instance the medical staff chose to impose the treatments they thought best without taking steps to find out about the patient's own interpretation of events. Attempting to explain to themselves the strength of Mrs. Hwa's reaction to having the blood tests done, and perhaps influenced by her age and lack of ability to communicate, they ended up understanding her behavior as indicating a psychiatric problem, despite her lack of any history of such problems. In fact, as Donnelly explains, for the Korean patient it was "inconceivable that the wishes of an elderly person would be ignored," and so it was deeply disturbing when tests whose purpose she did not understand were forced on her. Furthermore, the medical staff "did not realize that Asians, in particular, tend to have a severe reaction from neuroleptic medications."[44] Patients are far more than interchangeable organisms, and need to be treated accordingly.

Education

A colleague recently asked me what I thought about a problem he was having with a student in his class. When writing the syllabus he had decided to award a substantial portion of the credit for the course for participation in class discussions. He had noticed that a Korean student was not participating and had warned her in private conversation that her grade would suffer if she did not take part in discussion. Her level of participation did not rise significantly, and towards the end of the semester the student found herself faced with a low grade. Upset, she went to see the professor, who was now wondering what the right response should be. He understood that participation in discussion was uncomfortable for the student and that it was not a pattern of classroom behavior that she was used to in her home culture. On the other hand, he felt that he had been quite clear and explicit about the requirements of the course and that a student who chose to study in the United States had a responsibility to learn how to adapt to what was expected in a North American classroom. The student's concern that a low grade would be too shameful for her to tell her family about seemed like special pleading.

The problem was caused by a clear conflict in cultural values, with the result that there may be no simple solution. There is surely some justification to the idea that when visiting another culture, one has to learn to adapt to the norms of that culture in one's daily interactions, or else risk being penalized in various ways for not fitting in. At the same time, my colleague may have underestimated how difficult it can be to adjust cultural patterns of behavior instilled from an early age, especially when (as in this case) they are bound up with a gut level sense of respect, familial duty, shame, and being "good" in class, feelings that are more associated with deference and obedient listening than with vigorous discussion in traditional Korean education. To complicate matters further, some research suggests that discussion may not be an equally good way of learning for students of all cultural backgrounds. One study found that requiring students to speak out loud while solving various problems had no effect on how European Americans performed but was detrimental to the performance of Asian and Asian American students.[45] This raises questions not only about what would best contribute to our Korean student's learning, but also (given the inclusion of Asian *Americans*) about what the norms of a U.S. classroom should be assumed to be.

Such struggles affect both learners and their teachers, and can be a significant source of frustration, especially since the greater power possessed by mainstream cultural norms makes it harder for other perspectives to be genuinely heard. This concern is far from being limited to international students. Lisa Delpit reports comments by an African American school principal concerning discussions of education in graduate classes that she attended:

> If you try to suggest that's not quite the way it is, they get defensive, then you get defensive, then they'll start reciting research.
>
> I try to give them my experiences, to explain. They just look and nod. The more I try to explain, they just look and nod, just keep looking and nodding. They don't really hear me. . . . It becomes futile because they think they know everything about everybody. What you have to say about your life, your children, doesn't mean anything. They don't really want to hear what you have to say.[46]

In the interests of justice and fairness, teachers need understanding of how their own and their students' cultural perceptions and identities may be reflected in behaviors, understandings, and interpretations of what is happening in class. Such learning has, not surprisingly, become a standard part of teacher education. As the above comments make clear, there is a need not only for some background knowledge gleaned from books, but for educators who have developed the ability to listen to and learn from those whose identity is different from their own.

It would be easy to continue generating examples of how intercultural learning is relevant to a wide and growing range of professions. The chances that you will spend the rest of your life interacting with, working alongside, and serving only those who share your cultural identity are vanishingly small. If you want your life to be shaped more like the Samaritan's love of neighbor than Abraham's self-serving negative impact on the court of Abimelek, then intercultural learning is part of the package.

In the light of this, we can return to the question of how intercultural learning relates to various callings. Having responded on its own terms to the suggestion that intercultural learning is mainly relevant to those whose career lies in overseas mission, it is time to query the terms of the question itself. The question assumes that my calling can be identified with my career, and that my learning should serve that career. However, alongside and underneath the various specific stations in life to which God may call us is a basic calling to follow Christ, which means loving God and loving my neighbor.[47] Intercultural learning and a willingness to learn how to love amid linguistic and cultural differences are as relevant to my church, my neighborhood, and my willingness to attend to those around me as they are to my professional plans or aspirations.

If we only see and speak to people who look and sound like us, that often has more to do with the boundaries we have drawn for ourselves (or others have drawn for us) and the choices we or our social group are making about who to be with, than with the absence of possibility. A world in which "foreigners" live in distant lands reachable only by weeks of travel and are encountered only by a dedicated handful of career missionaries has long since disappeared; cultural difference is all around us. Intercultural learning should be seen as benefiting more than my career plans. Today, more than ever, loving the stranger is not a specialist career. It is a matter of Christian discipleship.

CHAPTER 6

LEARNING FROM THE STRANGER

Thus far we have explored the nature of cultural differences and the way they both form and arise from our ways of being in the world. We have also considered how Jesus' call to radical love of our neighbor, even when that neighbor is a cultural stranger, both offers a basic Christian reason for engaging with members of other cultures and suggests that some of our common approaches fall short. In the present chapter we will look more closely at some of the processes involved in learning to approach another culture with considerate responsiveness.

My aim in this chapter is not to give a complete, step-by-step guide to intercultural learning. Various existing books already attempt that task.[1] I do want to provide a basic sense of what is involved in learning to engage another culture, but I want to do so within a specific frame. My concern in this chapter will be to look at the relevant learning processes in terms of their relationship to Christian discipleship. I will be suggesting throughout (as I have been at least implicitly from the outset) that the relationship between intercultural learning and Christian faith is not merely an instrumental one. In other words, to think of intercultural learning simply as a tool that one learns how to use in order to later get to certain faith-related goals, such as missionary travel or church outreach, is too limited and too limiting. I suggest rather that intercultural learning can be grounded in Christian discipleship (as an outgrowth of a determination to love one's neighbor), and can itself be an arena of growth in Christian discipleship (as a way of becoming the kind of person who is more likely to love his or her neighbor). Intercultural learning is not just a means to a later end, but can itself be a process that encourages and involves spiritual growth; that is the core idea that focuses this chapter.

So what is involved in intercultural learning and what does it have to do with Christian maturity? We will look in turn at three phases of intercultural encounter: the before, the during, and the after. Before actual encounter we will ideally have engaged in some relevant learning in order to increase our chances of being a blessing rather than a curse to those we encounter. During the encounter we need to be able to draw on ways of hearing well, responding considerately, and being a loving presence. And after the encounter we need to find ways of integrating what we have learned into our identity as evidence that the other has been a real presence in our life. This is not an invariable sequence, of course, or one that just happens once and is done. Intercultural engagement is an ongoing spiral in which one encounter becomes part of what one knows before the next. In real life, moreover, the encounter may come first and be the thing that convicts us of the need for some learning. What follows is therefore not a fixed sequence but a loose framework within which to think about the processes involved.

Some Useful Kinds of Knowledge

While life can and does thrust strangers into our lives without a moment's notice, intentional intercultural encounters involve some prior preparation. If the planned encounter involves significant travel, there are familiar kinds of preparation that come easily to mind — finding out about currency rates, transportation schedules, likely weather conditions, availability of accommodation, and so on. Few people are content to simply hop on a plane without at least some basic research about where they are going. This kind of information gathering does not, however, move us beyond the tourist level of expertise. There are at least four other kinds of learning that are needed to help us engage more seriously with cultural others, whether at home or abroad.

The first arises from the fact that everyday conversation assumes a set of shared mental reference points and historical experiences. Our conversations are peppered with assumed knowledge of the world around us, ranging from the name of the local football team (and its recent record) to the names and positions of key political leaders, current TV shows, the kinds of activities that one is expected to have engaged in over the weekend, the locations (and reputations) of certain local streets and landmarks, and so on.

This assumed web of knowledge is almost invisible to us until it is taken away. I recall thinking when I moved from England to Canada that for someone who had lived in Germany the move to another English-speaking country would be pretty easy. I think it was that feeling that things ought to be straightforward, perhaps coupled with the fact that I was there for graduate study and was therefore supposed to be smart, that heightened the sense of sudden near-total ignorance. I would stand in front of rows of what were clearly large and popular stores and have no idea what kinds of things they sold until I peered through the windows or went inside. Insiders have learned, and forgotten that they have learned, that "Dominion" is a supermarket and "CIBC" is a bank, but the names of stores are rarely self-explanatory. I would want something and not know which store to visit to find it. In some cases I would not know what the item was called here, leaving me having to describe simple everyday objects to bemused store employees (which I would call "shop assistants") when my British words for things drew a blank. I would find myself having to read descriptions on packets of items to find out what they were whenever the brand name meant nothing to me and the package design was unfamiliar. My children would ask me the names of birds and trees in my "yard" (which I called my "garden"), and I would have no idea, reduced to parental ignorance by being faced with new species. I would find myself unable to interpret public signs — the sign posted at bus stops that said "No Standing" puzzled me for quite some time, for the verb "stand" is not commonly used of cars in England, only of people. I would ask for directions and not understand them, not being familiar with the taken-for-granted reference points. Listening to the radio, I had no idea who was being interviewed, or whether certain bands were famous, up-and-coming, or obscure. Watching comedy shows, I would get few of the jokes, and none of the ones involving the quirks and behaviors of politicians or media celebrities. Even in more serious discussions of current affairs it was hard to get a sense of what was at stake without any grasp of preceding events and local concerns. Until I began to adjust, life was a perpetual state of bewilderment, all the more disconcerting because it concerned simple things that I ought to know. Cross the ocean: become an ignoramus.

The obvious remedy here is some basic factual learning. Such learning covers both "high culture" and "low culture" — who is in power, and who is in fashion? What have been the major events of the last few decades, and what have been the talking points this year? How do people worship, and how do they shop? What is held sacred, what is taboo, and what is funny? Where are the major cities and where are the best cafés? Lest this become mere trivia quiz fodder, attention needs to be directed to the why as well as the what. Why have these particular cultural features emerged? What beliefs and values have shaped them? What do they show about what is most important to those who have played a role in shaping them? What beliefs and commitments are influencing the continuing development of the culture being studied? Relevant sources include scholarly volumes, newspapers, novels, movies, and popular music. All are more easily available at the present time than they have ever been — if the Internet does not solve the issue of intercultural learning, it at least broadens the range of raw material that can be quickly accessed. Acquiring even a basic range of political, geographical, historical, and cultural information increases one's ability to hold intelligent conversation. It also allows one to demonstrate respect by showing that one has made the effort to learn about the other's world. Simply taking an interest is a first step toward loving one's neighbor.

Second (and here the most useful sources are likely to be more specialized books and articles), it is helpful to have some awareness of the norms that govern interaction in the target culture. Are there invisible rules about who touches whom (should women shake hands with men?), what topics are avoided in conversation (is talk about money taboo?), what silences are observed (is interrupting a speaker normal?), what certain gestures mean (which fingers can and can't be raised in polite company?), and so on. Obviously a grasp of at least the basics in this area will mark the difference between appearing tactful or coming across as clumsy and perhaps even offensive. It will also have a bearing on how pleasant or otherwise one's own experiences in the new cultural setting are. Shortly after I arrived in Canada my landlady offered me a ride to the supermarket. When I got out of the car she called, "See you later!" and drove off. I had not been expecting a ride home. However, in my home speech community that phrase would tend to indicate that the person uttering it really expects to see me later, and so after shopping I waited outside the supermarket (in the snow!) for quite some time before daring to walk home. (My landlady was of course already there, and had simply been saying goodbye.)

Each year some of my students go to study in Germany for a semester. Those who stay in German university dormitories have to learn, sometimes painfully, that they will not automatically be invited to accompany groups going out to eat or watch a movie — but that it is quite acceptable to ask to go along; if they stay locked in their own interaction patterns the result can be many lonely evenings. As we have seen in various other examples in previous chapters, people do not interact the same way in different communities; some advance learning can go a long way toward smoothing the way.

Third, there are skills of intercultural communication that can be practiced, such as the skill of identifying and repairing breakdowns in communication due to cultural differences, the skill of discovering the knowledge one needs to navigate a new culture, whether from people or from other information sources, and the skill of interacting respectfully. Among the most important of these skills are language skills; wherever cultural differences are accompanied by different languages, language learning is vital. As some of the examples just mentioned show, even when English is the shared language, some awareness of differences in usage and meaning can be helpful. In many cases, however, English is not the local language and learning the other's language becomes a central way of communicating respect. In many cases, it is a precondition for being able to interact at all. I will not repeat here the discussion from the last chapter of the problems inherent in complacently relying on English for one's communication needs; at this point I will simply note that learning a language is a significant, demanding, but rewarding investment. While it is clearly not possible for an individual to learn all, or even many, of the world's languages (there are over six thousand), this is not much more of an obstacle than the equally true fact that it is not possible for an individual to marry all of the world's potential spouses or feed all of the world's children. Language learning, like love, always has to happen in concrete ways. The choice of language to learn will depend on a variety of factors, including existing ties to speakers of that language, ease of access to populations that speak it, opportunities opened up by it, and the question of which cultural groups one plans or expects to interact with most extensively. Once such matters have been considered, one has to simply begin at the beginning.

Particularly in North America there are many speakers of English who have consciously or subconsciously concluded that learning another language is beyond them, whether because of defective past learning experiences, over-expectation regarding the speed of results, or the widespread (but false) cultural belief that monolingualism is the normal lot of human beings. Prominent linguist Dell Hymes argues that the following list of beliefs represents common mainstream assumptions about language in the United States:

- Everyone in the United States speaks only English, or should.
- Bilingualism is inherently unstable, probably injurious, and possibly unnatural.
- Foreign literary languages can be respectably studied, but not foreign languages in their domestic varieties (it is one thing to study the French spoken in Paris, another to study the French spoken in Louisiana).
- Most everyone else in the world is learning English anyway, and that, together with American military and economic power, makes it unnecessary to worry about knowing the language of a country in which one has business, bases, or hostages.[2]

Such beliefs may be widespread, but that does not make them linguistically well-grounded. As another commentator points out, "Each of these assumptions is fundamentally flawed. The list as a whole is grounded in a lack of understanding of the nature of language, confuses historical mythology with historical fact, and is replete with both factual and normative errors."[3] In reality, a large portion of the world's population grow up at least bilingual, the majority do not speak English, many operate daily in several languages (and in varied versions of those languages), and while there are differences in aptitude, and therefore in the speed at which language will be acquired, the vast majority of people are entirely capable of acquiring a second language.

It does, of course, take effort. Despite the various magazine advertisements and quick-fix CDs promising near-instant results, the truth is that achieving fluency in a new language will take many hours of work and a degree of self-discipline. However, the rewards of being able to communicate with others in their own tongue, to directly access what they are saying and writing, and to thereby demonstrate respect for them in a very concrete manner can be enormous. As many travelers will testify, even very imperfect speech in another's language is often taken as a sign of good will and can open doors to rewarding interactions and relationships.

A fourth relevant kind of knowledge is found not in the target culture but in myself. The likelihood of being a blessing as a stranger when visiting another's cultural space is decreased if there is a lack of self-awareness on the part of the visitor. Many of my own cultural habits and expectations are invisible to me, part of the water in which I swim, until I begin to engage in the kinds of learning already described and become able to make comparisons. Becoming conscious of my own cultural ways of being, and of the impression that they are likely to make upon others who do not share them, can be an important step towards intercultural sensitivity. When I travel to Germany with students from the college where I teach, I always point out to them before I leave that the volume of conversation in public spaces is on average louder in Grand Rapids than in Germany. If my U.S. students walk the streets and ride the buses in Germany talking at their accustomed volume, they attract stares as the loudest people in the vicinity and risk reinforcing some European stereotypes of U.S. Americans. Female students from some areas of the U.S. need to learn before visiting certain parts of the world that their habit of making eye contact and smiling broadly when passing strangers may be pleasant and affirming in its home context but risks serious misinterpretation in many other cultural settings.

If I am used to strict timetables and have the value of punctuality deeply ingrained in my value system, I need to be aware that there are other cultural settings where time is experienced differently, and that I am likely to become frustrated with people in those settings despite the unreasonableness of holding them accountable to the temporal customs of my own community when I am in theirs. If there have been substantial past or present interactions between the cultural group that I represent and the one with which I hope to engage, knowing about them and their effects will be essential, for I may meet with reactions rooted in past injustices suffered at the hands of those with whom I am identified. I need to know who I am in terms of intercultural perception by virtue of being a member of my country and my ethnic group. My country's past and present military actions and cultural exports, my ethnic group's past or present ways of treating other ethnic groups, and people's past experiences of individuals whose cultural identity resembles mine will all form part of the context within which new encounters take place. Realizing this can be essential to achieving sensitivity and avoiding fresh miscommunication. Developing cultural self-awareness will also help me to explain aspects of my own culture in a more relevant and sensitive way. It is worth reflecting on the fact that to some degree I will through my behavior and utterances help to condition future attitudes towards the next person like me who is encountered. In addition to such specific items, a broader honest appraisal of one's own ability to suspend judgment, tolerate ambiguity, and act graciously in the face of the unexpected is also helpful preparation.

The kinds of learning that help prepare for intercultural encounter thus include learning information about the other culture, but also considerably more. Gaining an awareness of the hidden rules of another's culture, learning to speak in another's language, and growing in awareness of my own cultural ways and how they are perceived by others all play a role. This may seem a daunting list (and certainly we are talking about a serious task), but the goal is not a perfect command of the culture that I am going to encounter, just enough to make a space for dialogue to begin. The aim is to be able to behave well as an outsider, to be a blessing as a stranger, not to know everything the native knows. In fact, fruitful encounters involve learning to know less as well as to know more.

SOME USEFUL KINDS OF IGNORANCE

Paradoxical as it may seem, intercultural learning requires not only acquiring certain kinds of knowledge, but also cultivating certain kinds of ignorance. Understanding cultural others too quickly can be a problem, especially when we "understand" before we have really listened. This kind of premature understanding can happen in several ways. Perhaps the most common response to new experiences is to immediately seek to integrate them into our existing frameworks and schemes of knowledge. Discussing Marco Polo's renowned world travels, Umberto Eco comments that "when Marco Polo traveled to China he was obviously looking for unicorns."[4] What Polo knew about the world included the facts that unicorns existed and that they could be found in far-off, exotic countries. In Java he saw an animal with a single horn on its snout, and naturally came to the swift conclusion that he had seen a unicorn. He was honest enough to report that unicorns did not look the way the stories described them: instead of being white and graceful, they were black and had a head like a boar and feet like an elephant. Even though various aspects of the visual evidence did not fit, however, he adapted what he saw to his existing category of "unicorn" rather than admitting that he had seen a hitherto unknown animal, in fact a rhinoceros. Eco comments that Polo "could only refer to what he already knew and expected to meet. He was a victim of his background books."[5]

As we saw in Chapter 2, our cultural identities and experiences function as "background books" that condition how we interpret the world around us. When we encounter behaviors that are foreign to us, the temptation is great to immediately interpret them in terms of our own existing categories, even if some squeezing and trimming has to take place to make them fit. This gives us the security of feeling that we understand what is going on (most people do not enjoy being bewildered for long). However, it does so at the expense of operating on the basis of quick and probably inaccurate judgments that very easily come to have an undertone of moral approval or disapproval. Duane Elmer tells the story of a young Asian woman visiting the United States who was riding in a crowded train. Feeling tired, she rested her chin on the shoulder of a man standing in front of her, a stranger. His reaction quickly told her that this behavior was not as normal here as in her home country.[6] If you had witnessed this interaction, how would you have "understood" it?

Sometimes our easy assumption that we understand arises not from interpreting the strange too quickly, but from assuming too quickly that what we are seeing is familiar. In her vivid and moving account of the dramas arising from intercultural communication difficulties between Hmong refugees and Californian medical services, Anne

Fadiman describes conversations with local doctors about those difficulties. She asked one doctor why he and his colleagues had never
bothered to ask what traditional Hmong forms of medicine were being
applied at home in addition to, or instead of, the medications prescribed at the hospital. The doctor explained that

> because the Hmong dressed at least approximately in American
> clothes, had driver's licenses, and shopped in supermarkets, it
> never occurred to his colleagues — and only rarely to him — that
> they might practice esoteric healing arts. "If you went down to the
> rain forest and talked to the Yanomamo," he said, "you'd be sur-
> prised if they *didn't* come up with all sorts of fantastic spirit stories.
> You'd be surprised if they sat there and started saying, you know,
> 'where is the penicillin for my impetigo?' But if you took them to
> this setting, the way the Hmong have come here, and you dressed
> them up and they drove a car and came to [the hospital], you
> wouldn't expect to hear those spirit stories any more."[7]

Primed to look for the exotic as a mark of cultural difference, we can be
too quick to assume sameness on the basis of surface appearances. We
look, we see familiar sights, and we think we know what we need to
know.

Such premature understanding can even arise from some genuine learning about another culture. If I am accustomed to the idea that
time spent in class leads to secure and generalizable knowledge about
the world, and I have invested time in learning about the ways of another culture, I may be tempted to feel that now I have the key to understanding every member of that culture. Individual representatives
of the new culture are now expected to conform to the broad generalizations learned about in the sources. Here we are right back into the
realm of stereotypes, even if they have some limited validity. Of course
the reality is that generalizations about any cultural group are not natural laws, but statements that hold loosely for aggregate populations
but may not hold well for any given individual. Cultures are not monolithic blocks; individuals vary and cultural patterns are in a constant
state of change. Barbara Carvill tells the story of visiting China having
already learned that tipping bus boys in hotels is not customary in that
country. What she found was that the Chinese she encountered had

come to expect American hotel guests to give a tip and were disappointed if they did not.[8]

Problems can thus arise not only from our reliance on our own frames of reference, but also from over-applying what we think we know about another culture, instead of holding it lightly and keeping ourselves open to being surprised by the reality we encounter. Approaching someone with the assumption that we already understand them ahead of any conversation places them in our preconceived box and communicates no expectation that their own perspective might be important. This amounts to a failure to listen.

Instead of merely integrating the other into our own conceptual framework, it is crucial, Zali D. Gurevitch suggests, to be able to *not* understand:

> The ability to not understand is the ability to recognize and behold the other (or the self) as an other. In a moment of not understanding, what had been considered "understood" is relinquished as mere image. . . . When the other is perceived as strange, he or she is liberated from the image that one has projected onto the other's experience from the center of one's self. The other then emerges as an independent and "distant" phenomenon.[9]

In other words, to allow someone to be their own self in our presence involves holding back on our tendency to leap to conclusions and judgments and allowing the other to say things that may not fit our preconceptions, even our informed ones.

SOME WAYS OF GROWING SPIRITUALLY

In this interplay between knowledge and ignorance we can begin to see connections with the processes of spiritual growth. Such prominent New Testament themes as the tendency to judge others, humility, and the value that we place on others as compared to ourselves become directly relevant.

Another way to look at the conscious refusal to understand too quickly is to see it as disciplining ourselves to not judge prematurely. "Do not judge, or you too will be judged," said Jesus. "For in the same way you judge others, you will be judged" (Matthew 7:1). Jesus does not appear to be talking here about every kind of interpretation or misinterpretation that we might make; judging that my shirt is worn out, that I would be lying to make a certain statement, or even that torture is evil are not what is being challenged. His focus seems to be particularly on those judgments that paint another as a sinner who is beneath us and needs correction and repentance more than we do. At least some of the quick judgments that we make in the context of cultural difference are of this nature. We easily rush to interpreting cultural differences in moral terms (a different relationship to time becomes laziness, more direct forms of speech become arrogance, protracted silences become sullenness, indirectness becomes avoiding the issue, and so on). Learning to spot my own judgmental reactions to cultural others, cautioning myself to put them back on the shelf (perhaps through conscious self-talk: "Wait a minute, don't be so hasty!"), and suspending judgment for long enough to really find out what is going on are disciplines that offer a very practical training in not judging others.

This lands us in the neighborhood of cultivating humility. "Be completely humble and gentle," writes Paul, "bearing with one another in love" (Ephesians 4:2), and in another place: "Do nothing out of selfish ambition or vain conceit. Rather, in humility value others above yourselves" (Philippians 2:3). This is directly applicable both to learning in general and to intercultural learning in particular. Mark Schwehn tells the story of an occasion when he had assigned a text by Augustine to a college class. The students concluded from a quick reading of the text that Augustine was just obscure and mistaken, and dismissed the passage as unworthy of further attention. Acknowledging that he may have failed as a teacher to motivate them, Schwehn nevertheless argues that:

> My students could have overcome my failings had they been sufficiently humble; had they presumed that Augustine's apparent obscurity was their problem, not his; and had they presumed that his apparent inconsistencies or excesses were not really the careless errors they took them to be. Humility on this account does not mean uncritical acceptance: it means, in practical terms, the presumption of wisdom and authority in the author.[10]

Without at least some of this kind of humility we are unlikely to get very far in breaking through our own horizons of expectation. The same is true of learning another's language. Language learning involves stepping down from my secure sense of mastery when I speak in my mother tongue and submitting to a process that is at times clumsy, painful, and embarrassing, a process that at first reduces me to mangling unfamiliar sounds and stumbling over the simplest utterances. It involves gradually and laboriously learning to imitate another's ways of speaking, and patiently working to understand what they are saying. In learning to speak anew as well as in learning to interpret anew, "some degree of humility is a precondition for learning."[11]

Refusing to judge and exercising humility create space for the other to really enter our personal space. They enable the Christian practice of hospitality to strangers, a practice that "integrates respect and care."[12] "Do not forget to show hospitality to strangers," we are exhorted in Hebrews 13:2, "for by so doing some people have shown hospitality to angels without knowing it." Jesus lists welcome for strangers as one of the marks distinguishing the sheep from the goats in his parable of final judgment, indicating its importance as a New Testament virtue (Matthew 25:35). Hospitality to strangers includes literal provision of food and lodging when needed, but it also goes well beyond that to a broader commitment to welcoming behavior.[13] Hospitality implies

> that the stranger not only will be greeted, but also will be given loving attention. The stranger not only will be fed and given drink; his or her voice also will be granted space. His discomfort will be met with concern, her stories will be heard and responded to. . . . All of us have experienced the difference between homes where we are merely greeted with carefully measured civility and those in which we are genuinely welcomed, where there is authentic give and take. Maintaining a hospitable attitude means that we receive the representative of the target culture graciously and with love, and that we make space within ourselves for the stories and experiences he or she brings us from that culture.[14]

This practice of Christian hospitality offers a framing goal for the kinds of learning described earlier. Learning about another culture can become an exercise in intelligence gathering so as to secure my own advantage, or in collecting exotica to add to my mental museum of interesting facts, or in filling notebooks and polishing my brain in order to enhance my academic or economic prospects, or in listing comparisons that always end with the conclusion that my own ways are better. At least some of these motives have their place, but they may have little to do with love of God or neighbor. However, the same learning can be part of a process of making space within ourselves for others by attending respectfully and open-heartedly to their stories and experiences. When this happens, even book learning can become a way of practicing "care taken with the lives and thoughts of others."[15] Such learning becomes fitting preparation for the kinds of direct encounter with others that show love of my neighbor.

Encountering Cultural Others

At some point in all of this will come times of actual face-to-face encounter, times rich with possibility to yield new insights, connections, and friendships — or new stereotypes, suspicions, and discomforts. All of the kinds of learning already described may continue during the encounters. Such encounters test our ability to demonstrate considerate attentiveness and reveal how well we have cultivated attitudes of humility and hospitality. What concrete shape they take will vary widely. Here I want to underline two very simple suggestions: ask questions and pay attention.

In her account, mentioned above, of the Hmong community's difficulties relating to medical services in California, Anne Fadiman describes her difficulties and anxieties when first attempting to develop contacts with Hmong families. She had already researched Hmong culture and history and now needed personal contacts. Local doctors assured her that the families she wanted to interview mistrusted North Americans, were unwilling to communicate, and were difficult to relate to. Her preparatory reading about Hmong culture had given her a long list of possible cultural mistakes that she was anxious to avoid, ranging from removing shoes when entering homes to never offering to shake hands with a man for fear of implying loose morals. After some initial failed attempts to make contacts, Fadiman was helped by Sukey Walker, a local psychologist who had won the respect of the Hmong. A key piece of advice that Walker offered was that it was not necessary to "walk a razor's edge of proper etiquette" in constant fear of committing some grave cultural error. Walker explained:

> I've made a million errors. When I came here everyone said you can't touch people on the head, you can't talk to a man, you can't do this, you can't do that, and I finally said, this is crazy! . . . Now I have only one rule. Before I do anything I ask, Is it okay? Because I'm an American woman and they don't expect me to act like a Hmong anyway, they usually give me plenty of leeway.[16]

Asking respectful questions communicates concretely that I am willing to learn, and that I do not sit already secure in possession of all the relevant knowledge and expertise. Asking questions also signals, at least in principle, a willingness to listen to what the other has to say. For this reason, asking questions (again, as long as they are *respectful* questions) can be far more disarming than making statements, for it makes the questioner vulnerable and yields authority to the one questioned. Good questions communicate the willingness to not know and to learn from the other. I remind my language students from time to time that they are not learning a new language just so that they can bless more of the world with their opinions.

At the same time, paradoxically, good questions are rooted in prior learning. Questions that show complete naïveté and ignorance about the other's culture may simply be received as hilarious behavior on the part of a helpless outsider — but they can also come across as offensive, especially if put to relative strangers. Barbara Carvill gives examples of an American college student asking a forty-year-old gentleman in Spain in 1992 if he fought in the Spanish Civil War (thus implying that he was much older than he was), of American high school students asking German exchange students if Germans have refrigerators (they do), and of American travelers in Hungary asking the locals if they "knew Jesus" (leaving them in the angry belief that they had been accused of not knowing about Christianity).[17] Investing in some prior learning can enable one to ask questions that are appropriate and insightful, questions that show that one has already begun to think one's way into the other's culture and has respect for his or her context and experiences. Good questions are undergirded by an awareness of the historical context and an acceptance that the reasons why things might be as they are will be complex. Good questions can give the one questioned the gift of a new audience for topics and experiences that may have become old news to his or her usual conversation partners. Such conversations can lead to fresh insight on both sides of the exchange. As Russian thinker Mikhail Bakhtin puts it, "We raise new questions for a foreign culture, ones that it did not raise itself; we seek answers to our own questions in it; and the foreign culture responds to us by revealing to us its new aspects and new semantic depths."[18]

Sincere questions imply that I really want to hear the answer, and am not just looking for ways to display my own knowledge. If the practice of asking good questions indicates a willingness to engage, attentiveness to another's words and ways is a central way in which care is fleshed out. Bakhtin comments that human experience has a "valued manifoldness," a kind of complexity that engages our values and resists being boiled down to simple answers or general formulae. For this reason, he suggests, the only thing that will enable us to really encounter what is there is "loving contemplation," for "lovelessness, indifference, will never be able to generate sufficient attention to slow down and linger intently . . . to sculpt and hold every detail and particular."[19] A major form that love takes in conversation is attentiveness, slowing down, working to hear past one's own agendas and expectations to what the other has to say. At the heart of intercultural learning is learning how to *hear.*[20]

Hospitality, humility, and hearing belong together. As we saw in Chapter 4, if they part ways, then the idea of hospitality easily becomes a new form of condescension in which I am always the host and the other is always my needy guest. A colleague told me the following story.[21] A relative of hers, a math professor, was teaching a statistics class, and one of his students, who was from India, was struggling. He arranged to meet with this student weekly for individual tutoring. The weather was quite warm, the office was very small, and the student sat very close to the professor, who began to find his personal odor strong and offensive. The student used no deodorant, no mouthwash, and no aftershave. But the professor was determined to be tolerant and said nothing. At the end of the semester, the student came by to thank the professor for his help, and then added in a somewhat ashamed manner that there was something he had to confess. He admitted that he had found it very difficult working with the professor in such close quarters because the smell of the professor's cologne, aftershave, deodorant, and mouthwash had been overpowering and offensive. That professor learned something that day about how he himself was a stranger, not just the tolerant (and powerful) host he liked to see himself as. He learned it by listening, even when what he heard was not comfortable, and not by staying in helping mode. Loving the stranger is not about putting up with the inferior ways of others; it involves realizing that I am a stranger too.

Miroslav Volf suggests that we think of such encounters with others as being like an act of embrace:

> In an embrace I open my arms to create space in myself for the other. Open arms are a sign that I do not want to be by myself only, an invitation for the other to come in and feel at home with me. In an embrace I also close my arms around the other. Closed arms are a sign that I want the other to become part of me while at the same time I maintain my own identity. By becoming part of me, the other enriches me. In a mutual embrace, none remains the same because each enriches the other, yet both remain true to their genuine selves.[22]

Opening one's arms in this way suggests childlike expectation. At the same time, an embrace is temporary and retains a sense of freedom. A strangling bear hug in which one party constricts the other's breathing or seeks to prevent escape, or a one-sided clasp in which the other's arms are pinned to his or her sides are not usually forms of hospitable embrace. In its peculiar combination of openness, vulnerability, intimacy, and freedom, a genuine embrace offers an image of what intercultural encounter could be at its best, moving us from learning *about* others to learning *from* them and finally learning *with* them.[23]

What if the other does not receive us with open arms? What if the encounter is overshadowed by the history of past abuses of power, or by present resentments? What if the other responds to us with accusations, or with cold indifference? These are real possibilities. Volf insists that they do not change the Christian's responsibility to respond with embrace, for the decisive point of reference is the cross of Christ:

> The cross is the giving up of God's self in order not to give up on humanity; it is the consequence of God's desire to break the power of human enmity without violence and receive human beings into divine communion. . . . Forgiveness is therefore not the culmination of Christ's relationship to the offending other; it is a passage leading to embrace. The arms of the crucified are open — a sign of a space in God's self and an invitation for the enemy to come in.[24]

The cross shows us Christ's "self-giving love which overcomes human enmity and the creation of space within himself to receive estranged humanity."[25] If we desire to receive that love and enter that space within the "eternal embrace" of the Trinity, there are implications for how we in turn respond to others:

> Inscribed on the very heart of God's grace is the rule that we can be its recipients only if we do not resist being made into its agents; what happens to us must be done by us. Having been embraced by God, we must make space for others in ourselves and invite them in — even our enemies.[26]

Intercultural encounters may be places where we encounter suspicion, mistrust, even outright hostility. Sometimes we, or those whom we in some way represent, will be the ones whose past wrongs have given rise to hate, and we will need to walk the road of repentance, seeking forgiveness from the other. Sometimes we will be the ones forgiving. Either way, how we respond will not only help to shape the future of the immediate relationship, but will also reveal the degree of our willingness to become agents of God's grace.

TRUTH AND CONSEQUENCES

Hospitality, humility, and hearing lead to change. Matthew, one of my students, told me the story of a trip during his summer vacation. He spent some time in Switzerland staying with a Swiss family. Early in his stay he offended his hosts because of his showering habits. It had not occurred to him that there was anything unusual about the way he showered, but to his hosts, used to thinking of water as a limited and expensive resource, his habit of leaving the water running for the entire duration of his shower seemed irresponsibly wasteful. Taken to task by the family, he quickly learned that correct procedure in this part of the world was to turn off the water while applying soap and then turn it back on to rinse at the end. This experience could have become just another travel anecdote, except that it did not end there. The experience set Matthew thinking about how he used water, and how that related to his concern about the natural environment. He came to the conclusion that his own ways were indeed wasteful, and he decided to continue to shower in more economical fashion after his return to the United States. He returned home with a sense of not only being enriched by new experiences but also corrected by them.

When I take students to unfamiliar cultural settings and have them write about their experiences, I particularly look for these moments. It is difficult to quantify the kinds of learning that take place on such trips, but I do notice patterns in what students write. A few do not get very far beyond superficial comparisons involving mostly visual differences — the color of buses and mailboxes, styles of clothing, architectural differences, and the like. Others get further, making comparisons that show some insight into the values and life patterns of the new cultural setting, but show a tendency when making comparisons to always end up concluding that the different ways of the new setting are deficient when compared with home. Still others settle for a relativism that does not challenge their existing ways — they do things differently here, live and let live. However, the pieces of writing that seem to me to show the most evidence of real engagement are those in which a student has not only gained an understanding of local patterns of thought and behavior, but has begun to wrestle with whether this challenges any of his or her familiar ways of being in the world.

Taking off one cultural practice and putting on another is not in and of itself Christian repentance. Repentance is a turning away from one's sins and toward God, not just a change of cultural furnishings. But there are two ways in which allowing oneself to be transformed by intercultural encounter can become a part of repentance. First, the process often involves a laying down of pride, a confession that I was wrong, a setting aside of initial unjust judgments made about others, and a removing of the plank from my own eye. Genuine hospitality, argues Amy Oden, shifts the frame of reference from self to other to relationship. This shift invariably leads to repentance, for one sees the degree to which one's own view has become the only view. . . . When we realize how we have inflated our own frame of reference and imposed it on all of reality, we know we have committed the sin of idolatry, of taking our own particular part and making it the whole.[27]

Second, while many cultural differences are simply legitimate differences that can happily coexist, if I am attentive then there will be occasions when what emerges is not merely a fresh experience, but a challenge to change my life in ways that could lead to greater justice, compassion, and holiness. Not all differences are innocent. "Our coziness with the surrounding culture," writes Miroslav Volf, "has made us so blind to its many evils that, instead of calling them into question, we offer our own version of them — in God's name and with a good Christian conscience."[28] Sometimes gaining another perspective from outside our familiar frame of reference can give us eyes to see what needs to change. Both laying aside my pride and allowing my life to be reshaped by God's voice, wherever I hear it, belong to Christian repentance proper. Practice in such things is never a bad thing.

None of this implies that I need to swallow whole every new idea or practice that I encounter, or that I should rush to repentance every time a member of another culture disagrees with me. While Christians listen for their Shepherd's voice everywhere, they do not work on the assumption that it is the only voice out there. This is where another Christian practice becomes relevant, the practice of discernment. Discernment requires time and care invested in the attempt to avoid on the one hand concluding too quickly that my dislikes are God's judgments, and on the other hand being tossed around by every wind that blows. Often perceptions will change over time, as experience and insight are gained.

Since moving to the United States eight years ago I have been caught up in this process on multiple fronts. For instance, as a British person moving to the Midwest my first impression was a mixture of pleasure and puzzlement at the apparent avalanche of greetings of the "How are you doing?" or "Have a nice day!" variety that I encountered. On the one hand it was disconcerting (because culturally unfamiliar) to be greeted in this way by complete strangers such as store clerks; on the other hand it did give the distinct impression that everyone was very friendly. After a little while my perceptions turned negative, especially when I began to notice people asking me how I was doing as they walked past me without waiting for any response. The whole practice began to seem insincere, intrusive, and unwelcome. As more time has passed, however, and I have become acclimatized to the different emotional temperature of conversations here compared to where I came from, I have come round to thinking that even if it is often done unthinkingly, the social practice of wishing strangers well on a daily basis has a lot to be said for it in a world in which enmity seems to flare so easily. It is something I could be better at. It has taken time to get past initial reactions to what I hope is a more measured judgment.

At the same time, there are other aspects of the local culture to which I remain resistant. For example, watching the massive over-reliance on power tools for a range of yard work by people fit and healthy enough not to need them, tools that create excessive noise and unnecessary pollution in order to avoid a little effort that would provide healthy exercise, I continue to try to minimize my participation in such practices, which still seem to me to represent poor care of creation. Such judgments, which remain open to revision, concerning what to tolerate, what to actively embrace, and what to firmly but courteously resist are an ongoing part of encounter with any culture.

The consequences of intercultural encounter do not remain limited to my individual concerns. Insofar as I gain genuine understanding of more than one culture, I gain responsibilities as a mediator. It is virtually certain that there are those in my home culture who do not share my new understanding. There is no reason to think that they are required to learn everything that I learn, but my new understanding might put me in a position to bring some reconciliation when I encounter prejudice. When I return to England to visit friends and family, I am now in a position to help their perceptions of North Americans, which are not always positive and not always well-informed, to become more nuanced. Tempting as it is at times to fall in with familiar shared prejudices, my position as one who has lived in both cultures gives me the possibility and, I suggest, the moral obligation to speak up gently when false perceptions are aired.

Similarly, I impressed upon my students in German classes during the buildup to the U.S. invasion of Iraq, when the position of Germany and its reasons for not sending armed forces were being poorly represented in the local media, that their status as those able to read the German side of the story gave them new moral obligations as they discussed the war with friends, neighbors, and relatives in the U.S. Their new learning gave them the opportunity to be peacemakers by ensuring within their own small sphere of influence that German standpoints, often only fully accessible to those who could read German news sources, were fairly represented. As we encounter new cultural realities we become stewards of new knowledge, and the ways in which we speak of (or remain silent about) the cultural others whom we encounter can help spread peace or discord, understanding or prejudice. In some cases, a sense of obligation that is stronger yet may arise. Our learning and new relationships make us aware of injustices that had been hidden to us, past injustices that are still felt or injustices still being perpetrated. In those cases there may be a need for more than gentle corrections in everyday conversation; I may need to find more active ways of educating others and advocating change. "What does the LORD require of you?" asked the prophet Micah centuries ago. "To act justly," came the response, "and to love mercy and to walk humbly with your God" (Micah 6:8). "Blessed are the peacemakers," added Jesus, "for they will be called children of God" (Matthew 5:9). The outcomes of intercultural learning can go a long, long way beyond better answers on a test.

We began this chapter considering kinds of learning that everyone associates with classrooms — acquiring more information about history, geography, current affairs. As the chapter has progressed, I have sought to outline ways in which intercultural learning can become much more than this. It can be closely tied to the process of growth into Christian maturity. It can lead us to needed changes in our attitudes and behaviors. It can open us to the need to seek justice, love mercy, and walk humbly before God. None of these are inevitable accompaniments. It is entirely possible to keep intercultural learning within the bounds of the academic. It is equally possible to travel the world and sustain our prejudices throughout the experience. If we are willing, however, intercultural learning can be taken up into the work of redemption, the creation of a new people that began on the cross and erupted into the world at Pentecost. Learning from the stranger can be part of learning to live the life of faith.

CHAPTER 7

OF BABBLERS AND BARBARIANS

ACTS 2:5-12

Now there were staying in Jerusalem God-fearing Jews from every nation under heaven. When they heard this sound, a crowd came together in bewilderment, because each one heard their own language being spoken. Utterly amazed, they asked: "Aren't all these who are speaking Galileans? Then how is it that each of us hears them in our native language? Parthians, Medes and Elamites; residents of Mesopotamia, Judea and Cappadocia, Pontus and Asia, Phrygia and Pamphylia, Egypt and the parts of Libya near Cyrene; visitors from Rome (both Jews and converts to Judaism); Cretans and Arabs — we hear them declaring the wonders of God in our own tongues!" Amazed and perplexed, they asked one another, "What does this mean?"

ACTS 10:25-35

As Peter entered the house, Cornelius met him and fell at his feet in reverence. But Peter made him get up. "Stand up," he said, "I am only human myself."

While talking with him, Peter went inside and found a large gathering of people. He said to them: "You are well aware that it is against our law for a Jew to associate with Gentiles or visit them. But God has shown me that I should not call anyone impure or unclean. So when I was sent for, I came without raising any objection. May I ask why you sent for me?"

> Cornelius answered: "Three days ago I was in my house praying at this hour, at three in the afternoon. Suddenly a man in shining clothes stood before me and said, 'Cornelius, God has heard your prayer and remembered your gifts to the poor. Send to Joppa for Simon who is called Peter. He is a guest in the home of Simon the tanner, who lives by the sea.' So I sent for you immediately, and it was good of you to come. Now we are all here in the presence of God to listen to everything the Lord has commanded you to tell us."
>
> Then Peter began to speak. "I now realize how true it is that God does not show favoritism but accepts those from every nation who fear him and do what is right."

THE CROWD

The visitors were understandably amazed. They had not come to Jerusalem looking for novelty. Quite the opposite. They had come looking to take their place within the stable rhythms of rituals celebrated for centuries, to enact their own continuity with the people of God through time and space. Many had come from a long way off, some perhaps saving for years for a once-in-a-lifetime visit to the holy city. Some had arrived in time for Passover and stayed a month to celebrate Pentecost also. Children of the Jewish Diaspora, those scattered among the nations since Israel's exile, they had grown up in a range of other places and cultures. Their hometowns were for the most part Greek-speaking alongside local languages, but they still looked to Jerusalem as the geographic and symbolic center of their faith and identity. Some came yearly from places closer at hand, from various parts of Palestine itself, mostly speakers of Aramaic, but in many cases functionally bilingual: Greek and Aramaic were both current on the streets of Jerusalem. Those who had no relatives in Jerusalem were crowded into hostels provided for out-of-town visitors to the great festivals. Together, the various varieties of pilgrim not only swelled the population of Jerusalem, but also filled the area around the temple to capacity as the festival prayers were offered. They interacted with those around them in one or the other of their two shared languages.[1] As the feast of Pentecost began there was a sense of anticipation, not for novelty, but for a corporate celebration of the first fruits of the harvest that would affirm the true and enduring order of things: God in his temple and his people at thankful worship.

This year turned out to be not just different, but world-changing. First, raised voices were heard, snatches of prayer and praise carrying over the crowd. Nothing unusual in that, but when in a gathered multitude someone hears the language of home it catches their attention. A fellow pilgrim from Crete? Surely I know him, or we must have met on the journey. It's odd that I don't recognize the voice. Some turned to comment to their neighbors, and soon discovered that others were also hearing their own languages — in fact it seemed that each of those present could hear a voice in the local language of their homeland. This *was* unusual. What was happening? Some new kind of welcoming committee? Puzzlement deepened to outright perplexity when the explanation turned out to be even stranger than that which it was supposed to explain. The news spread through the crowd that those shouting the wonders of God in various languages were Galileans, yokels, unlettered rustic folk who could barely speak their own language without raising smirks from the sophisticated. Some locals identified them as followers of the latest

> Now there were staying in Jerusalem God-fearing Jews from every nation under heaven. When they heard this sound, a crowd came together in bewilderment, because each one heard their own language being spoken. Utterly amazed, they asked: "Aren't all these who are speaking Galileans? Then how is it that each of us hears them in our native language? Parthians, Medes, and Elamites; residents of Mesopotamia, Judea and Cappadocia, Pontus and Asia, Phrygia and Pamphylia, Egypt and the parts of Libya near Cyrene; visitors from Rome (both Jews and converts to Judaism); Cretans and Arabs — we hear them declaring the wonders of God in our own tongues!" Amazed and perplexed, they asked one another, "What does this mean?"
>
> ACTS 2:5-12

in a string of executed would-be Messiahs, last heard of skulking in disgrace after their leader was crucified. This wasn't an explanation — it was a just a set of new puzzles. Had they been drinking away their despair? But where did their sudden facility with languages come from? The visitors were understandably amazed.

THE SHAPE OF POWER

Pentecost is in various ways pivotal. Fitting chronologically right after the four evangelists' accounts of the death and resurrection of Jesus Christ, the particular day of Pentecost recorded in Acts stands at the beginning of the rest of history. Fulfilling Jesus' promise that on his departure he would send his Spirit to indwell his followers, this day of Pentecost is in a sense the full inauguration of the Christian church, the "beginning of the creation of God's eschatological people."[2] Bringing together fire, wind, and divinely empowered speech, the events at Pentecost evoke the breath/spirit of God at the creation of the world (Genesis 1), the fire and noise that heralded the giving of the law at Sinai (Exodus 19), the wind that breathed life into the dry bones in Ezekiel's vision of a renewed and restored Israel (Ezekiel 37), all suggesting that something of epochal significance is afoot.[3]

Nevertheless, Luke's account of the events of the first Christian Pentecost (Acts 2:1-4) is sparse in the extreme. The description of the initial miracle itself is a mere four verses long and cautious, even hesitant, in what it describes: there was something that *sounded like* wind, something that *looked like* fire — something remarkable but hard to pin down.[4] The dramatic quality of these events and their paradigmatic status as a framing moment for the emerging Christian church have, however, led to them becoming the stimulus for paintings, sermons, even whole theologies and denominations. It takes some effort to imagine what it might have been like for those present, people who had never read the New Testament (for not a word of it was yet written). What would it be like not to know the story, to have no expectation of the tongues like flame, the sound like wind, the linguistic miracle, just an anticipation of something new and powerful set in motion by the raising of God's anointed one from death?

The book of Acts begins with a conversation between the resurrected Jesus and his disciples immediately before his ascension (Acts 1:1-8). It seems that at that point in time the disciples' thoughts had turned back with renewed hope to the national restoration of a glorious and independent Israel. After their sense that Jesus was indeed the promised Messiah was first dashed by his crucifixion and then given fresh wings as he rose from the dead, their question to him was "Lord, are you at this time going to restore the kingdom to Israel?" (Acts 1:6). After the apparent defeat (now reversed) at the cruel hands of Roman justice, would Jesus now lead Roman-occupied Israel to liberation?

Jesus' response was enigmatic. He did not directly contradict their expectation of national renewal, but rather told them: "It is not for you to know the times or dates the Father has set by his own authority." All that he would add by way of instruction was that "you will receive power when the Holy Spirit comes on you; and you will be my witnesses in Jerusalem, and in all Judea and Samaria, and to the ends of the earth" (Acts 1:7-8).[5] And then he left them, to be seen no more. Not much to go on if you are trying to imagine what will happen next.

With hindsight we can see Jesus shifting the terms of their expectations — they are to be renewed as witnesses, not as potentates, and the renewal of God's people is to bring blessing to the nations and not just to Israel, as God had indicated to Abram long ago.[6] These words must have been debated during the meetings in the upper room in the days that followed. Which words resonated most seductively in their minds? "Power" or "witness"? "Judea" or "the ends of the earth"? That the first act of the disciples after Jesus' ascension is to restore the number of apostles to the symbolic number of twelve, echoing the twelve tribal leaders who

> So when they met together, they asked [Jesus], "Lord, are you at this time going to restore the kingdom to Israel?" He said to them: "It is not for you to know the times or dates the Father has set by his own authority. But you will receive power when the Holy Spirit comes on you; and you will be my witnesses in Jerusalem, and in all Judea and Samaria, and to the ends of the earth."
>
> ACTS 1:6-8

founded Israel, might suggest that the thought of national restoration remained uppermost in their minds. How did they imagine what would happen next, as they waited in a house in Jerusalem, held together by their common faith in Jesus and an obscure expectation of supernatural power?

Modern folk have their own standard cultural images of people

energized by power from on high. When someone is mysteriously infused with superhuman power, muscles bulge, shirts rip, and a former
weakling becomes able to hurl large vehicles across the street. For-
merly average legs become able to run alongside trains or leap from
building to building. Senses are sharpened, forewarning of impending
danger, and frail human flesh becomes virtually invulnerable to harm.
Supernatural power makes ordinary people faster, stronger, more invincible; it takes away their weakness and shame, and results in the defeat of their enemies. But that's Hollywood, hardly relevant to first-
century Jews. Surely their imaginations ran along different lines. After
all, it's the Holy Spirit, rather than gamma rays or radioactive spiders,
who is to bring the power in this story. Surely superhero images were
far from their minds as they waited in prayer.

Maybe. Or maybe not. These Jewish disciples had their own grip-
ping stories about how the Spirit of God came on people with power.
When Samson was attacked by a roaring lion, "the Spirit of the LORD
came on him in power so that he tore the lion apart with his bare hands
as he might have torn a young goat" (Judges 14:6). When he fell into debt
because of a lost wager, "the Spirit of the LORD came on him in power.
He went down to Ashkelon, struck down thirty of their men, stripped
them of everything and gave their clothes to those who had explained
the riddle" (Judges 14:19). And when his Philistine enemies encountered
him bound by two new ropes, "the Spirit of the LORD came on him in
power. The ropes on his arms became like charred flax, and the bindings
dropped from his hands. Finding a fresh jawbone of a donkey, he
grabbed it and struck down a thousand men" (Judges 15:14-15).

Later, when Saul heard of the humiliation being suffered by the
men of the besieged city of Jabesh Gilead, "the Spirit of God came on
him in power, and he burned with anger. He took a pair of oxen, cut
them into pieces, and sent the pieces by messengers throughout Israel,
proclaiming, 'This is what will be done to the oxen of anyone who does
not follow Saul and Samuel'" (1 Samuel 11:6-7).[7] The result was a crush-
ing defeat for the besieging Ammonites. Later still, as the sky grew
black after Elijah's triumph over the prophets of Baal on Mount Carmel,
"the power of the LORD came on Elijah and, tucking his cloak into his
belt, he ran ahead of Ahab all the way to Jezreel" (1 Kings 18:46) — with
Ahab, it should be noted, covering the twenty-five miles or so in a
horse-drawn chariot. When the Spirit of the LORD comes on ordinary

people with power, they are made faster, stronger, more invincible; their weakness and shame are removed and their enemies are defeated. With Israel still occupied by a foreign army, and the Messiah cheating Roman execution by rising from the dead, did any of this run through some of the minds of those who waited to "receive power"?

But perhaps others were thinking along different lines. Perhaps they had gained a better grasp of where Jesus' teaching was headed. Perhaps they had paid careful heed to the second part of Jesus' response to their last question to him: "You shall be witnesses . . . to the ends of the earth." Perhaps it put them in mind of other precedents from their heritage of faith. Samuel, for instance, giving Saul a promise remarkably similar to the one they had just heard: "You will go to Gibeah of God, where there is a Philistine outpost. As you approach the town, you will meet a procession of prophets coming down from the high place with lyres, timbrels, pipes and harps being played before them, and they will be prophesying. The Spirit of the LORD will come upon you in power, and you will prophesy with them; and you will be changed into a different person" (1 Samuel 10:5-6). Or Isaiah, prophesying about one who would "give decisions for the poor of the earth," for

> The Spirit of the LORD will rest on him —
> the Spirit of wisdom and of understanding,
> the Spirit of counsel and of might,
> the Spirit of the knowledge and fear of the LORD.
>
> (Isaiah 11:2)

Perhaps the power to prophesy to all people and raise up the poor, maybe with the miraculous accompaniments that bore witness to the power of the Spirit in Jesus' own ministry, was to the fore in the minds of the gathered disciples.[8]

THE LOVER OF MANKIND

Whatever their precise expectations, it is hard to see grounds for them to expect exactly what transpired on the day of Pentecost, and bewilderment is the response emphasized in Luke's account. It was not bewilderment at the wind-like sound or the flame-like manifestation of

God's presence so beloved of later artists. It is not even clear that the crowd saw these, as the action moves from the gathering in the upper room to the crowd outside before responses are recorded; by the time the crowd enter the story, the wind and fire are in the background. What bewilders the crowd (we are told this no less than four times) is hearing Galileans, not noted for their linguistic prowess, speaking different languages.[9] The arresting event is that each hears a message from Galilean lips, that the Spirit of God reaches out to each listener in his or her own mother tongue. The result of the Spirit of the LORD empowering his followers had never looked quite like this in any of the familiar stories, whether of the military might or prophetic authority varieties.[10] (To catch a sense of the oddity of this tale, consider an aspiring scriptwriter approaching a Hollywood studio with an idea for a new movie. A mild-mannered insurance salesman is exposed to strange cosmic radiation and undergoes mysterious changes. From that day forward, when times of crisis arise, he finds himself . . . able to speak Norwegian. How much would you invest in the script?)

> Utterly amazed, they asked: "Aren't all these who are speaking Galileans? Then how is it that each of us hears them in our native language? Parthians, Medes and Elamites; residents of Mesopotamia, Judea and Cappadocia, Pontus and Asia, Phrygia and Pamphylia, Egypt and the parts of Libya near Cyrene; visitors from Rome (both Jews and converts to Judaism); Cretans and Arabs — we hear them declaring the wonders of God in our own tongues!" Amazed and perplexed, they asked one another, "What does this mean?"
>
> ACTS 2:7-12

The linguistic fireworks seem not only surprising, but also gratuitous. It is easy to assume that the multiplication of tongues was an emergency miracle, designed to overcome language barriers and enable an immediate offer of salvation without having to wait for more pedestrian processes of language learning and translation. Two points count against that idea. First, according to the historians, people from the places listed in verses 9-11 would have been familiar with Aramaic or Greek.[11] Second, and more obvious from the text itself, as soon as the crowd is gathered Peter gets up and preaches a sermon to the assembled multitude. There is no suggestion that this sermon underwent miraculous translation, yet it is the response to the sermon that results in three thousand baptisms.[12]

Of course, with hindsight the surprise is not total. You will be a blessing to the nations, Abram was told by God, even if he fell short in his own first efforts. Love the alien as yourself, the Torah insisted. Love your neighbor as yourself, even if your neighbor is a Samaritan, Jesus echoed. In *everything*, do to others what you would have them do to you, love your enemies, lay aside the desire to be the center of your world and love as God loves, without favoritism. The events of Pentecost whisper further in the voice of the Spirit: "Even if you can get by in the common tongue, even if I could require you to master a second language in order to hear what I have to say, I am going to reach out to you on your terms, in your words, in the language that speaks to your heart." This is the ethical opposite of the all too common attitude that says, "I can get by with my own language, so there's no pragmatic need for me to learn anyone else's; if they want to hear what I have to say it will be on my terms, in my tongue."[13] The Babel project of Genesis 11, in which an imperial "one speech" seeks a self-centered security against God's command to spread and fill the earth, finds its redemptive counterpart as people hear one another anew, each in their own language.[14] As the Spirit begins to renew the people of God and manifest God's kingdom in and through them, what else should we expect by this point but genuine love for others in all their cultural and linguistic particularity? As an ancient poem by Ephrem the Syrian recognizes, Pentecost presents a divine act of hospitality:

> When the blessed apostles
> were gathered together
> the place shook
> and the scent of Paradise
> having recognized its home
> poured forth its perfumes,
> delighting the heralds
> by whom
> the guests are instructed
> and come to his banquet;
> eagerly he awaits their arrival
> for he is the Lover of mankind.[15]

The power that is given at Pentecost is not the power to conquer foreigners, but the power to speak to others in the way that they hear, the power to hear anew across lines of difference, the power to love one's neighbor as oneself.

WHO ARE THE PEOPLE OF GOD?

It soon becomes apparent that this is not just a curious episode, a one-time peak experience standing apart from the rest of Christian experience. It is more like an overture, sounding themes that will be unfolded further as we stay for the rest of the performance. What we see developing over the ensuing chapters is an ongoing transformation of the boundaries of the people of God, as the Spirit's primal act of Pentecostal hospitality echoes outward, starting at Pentecost itself.

The small body of believers gathered at Pentecost probably already contained some cultural diversity. David Fiensy explains that "the predominantly Jewish city of Jerusalem was bicultural. Most of the residents spoke and understood only Aramaic; some were bilingual; still others could probably speak only Greek." In Jerusalem, "Aramaic was predominant. . . . Yet many, especially the educated and merchants, did learn Greek either out of an interest in Greek literature, a desire to appear sophisticated, or for business reasons." Some (perhaps ten to twenty percent of the population) were native speakers of Greek who had moved to Jerusalem from Diaspora locations.[16] That these differences were reflected in the early church is clear from Acts 6:1-6, where we find a dispute arising within the church between the Hellenistic (i.e., Greek-speaking) and the Hebraic Jews.[17] Thus, "although the early Jerusalem church was entirely Jewish, it was nonetheless socially and culturally pluralistic."[18] From its very inception the Christian church was figuring out how to sustain fellowship amid differences of language and culture.

The day of Pentecost put this process on steroids. At Pentecost, hundreds of thousands of pilgrims, most from Palestine but perhaps as many as 30,000 from the Greek-speaking Diaspora, swelled the population of Jerusalem to several times its usual size. Luke emphasizes (at greater length than his description of the wind and fire) that the crowd gathered at Pentecost was drawn from nations all around the Mediterranean, and included both ethnic Jews belonging to the Diaspora (those scattered among the nations following Israel's exile) and those of other ethnicities who were Jews by conversion.[19] The crowd was both ethnically and culturally diverse, again with one limitation: they were all Jews. They were, after all, present to celebrate a Jewish festival, and Peter addresses them as fellow Israelites (Acts 2:14, 22, 36). The three thousand converts that result from his sermon expand the group of believers dramatically, and also now give it an international identity rooted in that of the scattered people of Israel.

As Luke's story continues to unfold, startling developments expand the circle further. It is not very long since Jesus' disciples were asking permission to call down fire on the heads of the degenerate Samaritans (Luke 9:54). In Acts 8 we find Philip preaching in "the city of Samaria" (Acts 8:5).[20] When the Jerusalem headquarters hears that Samaria has accepted the gospel, Peter and John are sent to investigate. The Samaritans receive the Spirit as the apostles pray for them and lay hands on them, and are thus shown to be full participants in the church based at Jerusalem. As Peter and John head for home, preaching in Samaritan villages along the way (Acts 8:25), "on the Christian side of the fence, Jew and Samaritan are now one people."[21]

> When the apostles in Jerusalem heard that Samaria had accepted the word of God, they sent Peter and John to Samaria. When they arrived, they prayed for the new believers there that they might receive the Holy Spirit, because the Holy Spirit had not yet come on any of them; they had simply been baptized into the name of the Lord Jesus. Then Peter and John placed their hands on them, and they received the Holy Spirit. . . . After they had further proclaimed the word of the Lord and testified about Jesus, Peter and John returned to Jerusalem, preaching the gospel in many Samaritan villages along the way.
>
> ACTS 8:14-17, 25

The sight of Jews and Samaritans praying together (not just talking on the street, but *praying* together) is a dramatic one, but Luke does not linger over it. Instead he takes us straight to Philip's next assignment: sharing the gospel with a stranger who is both a eunuch (and thus excluded from full participation in temple worship) and an Ethiopian (Acts 8:27). This Ethiopian official does not need to be treated like a blank slate — he is already meditating on Isaiah's prophecies. He too becomes a part of the emerging new people of God, fully included by baptism (Acts 8:38). In a single chapter, the boundaries of the church have expanded to include two former kinds of outcasts, Samaritans and eunuchs, fulfilling words spoken by Isaiah centuries earlier: "Let no foreigners who have bound themselves to the LORD say, 'The LORD will surely exclude me from his people.' And let no eunuch complain, 'I am only a dry tree'" (Isaiah 56:3).[22]

Heady stuff. What next? Luke races onward to the conversion of Saul, an outright enemy of the church, making no bones about Ananias's initial reluctance when he hears the call to seek out and pray with such a person. Saul, Ananias is told, is to proclaim the gospel to the Gentiles. Before going on to narrate the ministry of Saul (soon to be known as Paul), Luke steps sideways to give us a lengthy (and repeated) account of a peculiar but vital episode involving Peter (Acts 10).

Sitting on the roof waiting for lunch to be ready, Peter sees three times a vision of a cloth on which are various creatures, including ceremonially unclean animals that were forbidden to Jews as food. Three times a voice tells him to eat, an instruction that he finds shocking. Almost at once, three Gentile men approach and take him to the house of Cornelius, a Gentile and a centurion. The location now is Caesarea, not bicultural like Jerusalem, but very much multicultural. Caesarea was a place where Jews, Samaritans, and a variety of Gentiles lived and an array of religions were practiced — some rabbis referred to it as the "daughter of Edom" because of its paganism.[23] The centurion in question is a God-fearer, but not a convert to Judaism, and he is clearly a foreigner — "in the imagination of anyone listening to a story about a centurion, the centurion would always have had a Roman face."[24] Cornelius and his household believe and receive the Spirit before Peter has had the chance to decide whether to lay hands on them, and Peter realizes that "God does not show favoritism [literally, does not judge by appearances], but accepts men from every nation who fear him and do what is right" (Acts 10:34-35). As if Samaritans and eunuch converts were not already enough of a leap, the church now includes outright Gentiles and becomes open to those of any and every ethnicity.

It is worth imitating Luke and pausing over this story. A vision of animals on a tablecloth might seem a roundabout or even bizarre way of broadening Peter's horizons. In its context, however, it was an eloquently disturbing statement. The dietary laws followed by Jews, grounded in the provisions of the Torah, formed an important part of their sense of separate religious and ethnic identity, setting them apart from Gentiles as God's holy people. Willingness to share table fellowship with another person was (and still often is) an important marker of inclusion or exclusion.[25] Peter reminds Cornelius that "it is against our law for a Jew to associate with Gentiles or visit them" (Acts 10:28). He does not say that it was forbidden to talk to them. Jews and Gentiles could talk in public, and the Pharisees undertook missionary activity among Gentiles (Matthew 23:15) — preaching from a

> As Peter entered the house, Cornelius met him and fell at his feet in reverence. But Peter made him get up. "Stand up," he said, "I am only human myself." While talking with him, Peter went inside and found a large gathering of people. He said to them: "You are well aware that it is against our law for a Jew to associate with Gentiles or visit them. But God has shown me that I should not call anyone impure or unclean. So when I was sent for, I came without raising any objection. May I ask why you sent for me?"
>
> ACTS 10:25-29

safe distance was quite acceptable. What was out of the question was being in their homes and sharing meals with them — down that path lay defilement. When Peter told the story of Cornelius to the other believers in Jerusalem, he was immediately attacked not for preaching to Gentiles, or even for what he ate. The telling accusation was that "you went into the house of the uncircumcised and ate with them" (Acts 11:3).[26] Peter's vision is about a lot more than a balanced diet.

Earlier in Luke's account (which spans Luke and Acts), he recounted another story in which a centurion sent messengers requesting assistance (Luke 7:1-10). A valued servant of his was sick, and he believed that Jesus could heal him. That centurion was not quite as bold as Cornelius (but then he did not have the benefit of direct instructions from an angel). The nature of his caution speaks volumes. Instead of sending his own servants, he sent Jewish elders to speak with Jesus, hoping for a more sympathetic response to such a delegation. When Jesus responded and set out to visit the sick servant, the centurion sent further emissaries to reassure the Jewish rabbi that he did not expect him to actually enter his house — if Jesus just spoke the word of healing from a distance, that would suffice (7:7). Jesus was apparently quite prepared to go to the centurion's house, for the second message did not reach him until he was on his way there. However, he marveled at the centurion's faith and then honored his request, healing at a distance.

Peter is hit in quick succession by a vision that he does not fully grasp, but that clearly has to do with scruples about purity in connection with eating, and by a delegation from a centurion who wants Peter to visit.[27] The symmetries of the account of Peter's encounter with Cornelius are telling.[28] Both Cornelius and Peter receive visions while praying, preparing each to encounter the other; God speaks on both sides of the divide, without favoritism. When Peter hears the request of the three men, he does not hit the road at once, but rather invites them "into the house to be his guests" (Acts 10:23), not leaving until the next day. He shares food and accommodation with his Gentile visitors. This is a step in their direction, but does not risk as much uncleanness as staying in the house of a Gentile would — Peter still gets to be host. The next day, however, the events unfold at Cornelius's house,[29] and after the baptisms comes a balancing detail: "Then they asked Peter to stay with them for a few days" (10:48). The journey of the Gentile visitors and the welcome that Peter offers them are balanced by Peter's journey and the welcome he receives from the Gentiles. Now Peter is the guest, and must allow his Gentile hosts to minister to him, and not merely receive from him. Peter learns to imitate God's lack of favoritism by sharing food, shelter, and salvation with Gentiles in a manner that does not allow him to stay in the potentially condescending role of host. The Gentiles, too, receive a stranger and through *their* hospitality hear a word from the Spirit. The Jewish Pentecost of Acts 2 is now mirrored by a Gentile Pentecost as Cornelius and his household receive the Spirit and the gift of tongues.[30]

While both the divine message received by Cornelius and the subsequent events emphasize that Peter has a message that Cornelius needs to hear, the learning is not all on one side. The first vision is given to the Gentile who is not yet a disciple, and it meets with ready obedience (remember Abimelek?). It is Peter, not Cornelius, who resists and struggles to understand what the Spirit is telling him. He is still puzzling over the meaning of his vision when the messengers show up (Acts 10:19). Just as the Gentile messengers hesitated at the threshold of Peter's house when they arrived, Peter speaks aloud his qualms about associating closely with Gentiles as he enters the house of Cornelius (10:27-28).[31] Then it is Cornelius who gives the first speech, and Peter who listens. As he listens to Cornelius, he learns that an angel has actually been in the house before him (10:30; 11:13), and when his turn comes to speak the message is not one that he had in his grasp before he arrived. His opening words are "I now realize . . ." (10:14), and the tense

> Cornelius answered: "Three days ago I was in my house praying at this hour, at three in the afternoon. Suddenly a man in shining clothes stood before me and said, 'Cornelius, God has heard your prayer and remembered your gifts to the poor. Send to Joppa for Simon who is called Peter. He is a guest in the home of Simon the tanner, who lives by the sea.' So I sent for you immediately, and it was good of you to come. Now we are all here in the presence of God to listen to everything the Lord has commanded you to tell us." Then Peter began to speak. "I now realize how true it is that God does not show favoritism but accepts those from every nation who fear him and do what is right."
>
> ACTS 10:30-35

gives these words the sense that he is just now coming to this realiza-tion.[32] Peter only comes to fully understand the meaning of his own vision *after* he has heard Cornelius explain about his, and it is in the house of Cornelius that he gains a fuller sense of the gospel that he came to preach, a gospel that he then has to defend to the believers back in Jeru-salem.[33]

It is easy to imagine an alternative version (one that would better suit most of us) in which Peter, the great man of God, is told by the Spirit in a luminous vision that the Gentiles must be saved. He then magnanimously invites a nearby centurion to his house to hear the gospel explained, benefit from his benevolence, and be given a place as a graciously received but somewhat second-class citizen at his table. Something like that is not too far removed from the framework that al-ready existed for Gentiles becoming Jewish converts. That is not, how-ever, what we get. When Cornelius does cast himself down at Peter's feet as the latter arrives at his house, Peter lifts him up and assures him

that they are both just human beings. As with the conversion of Saul —
and as in Abraham's encounter with Abimelek — God speaks first to the
outsider (the pagan, the persecutor, the Gentile), it is the figure of faith
who is reluctant (Abraham, Ananias, Peter), and there is change and
learning that has to happen on both sides. In all three cases, each side needs the other to piece together what God is doing. Here in the story of Cornelius the centurion, the pointed symmetries indicate an expansion of the people of God through inclusion without condescension. Peter has to love the stranger as himself.[34] If you count yourself Christian and are not ethnically Jewish, you owe an enormous debt to these founding acts of mutual hospitality.

> So when Peter went up to Jerusalem, the circumcised believers criticized him and said, "You went into the house of the uncircumcised and ate with them." Starting from the beginning, Peter told them the whole story. . . . "As I began to speak, the Holy Spirit came on them as he had come on us at the beginning. Then I remembered what the Lord had said: 'John baptized with water, but you will be baptized with the Holy Spirit.' So if God gave them the same gift he gave us who believed in the Lord Jesus Christ, who was I to think that I could stand in God's way?"
>
> ACTS 11:2-4, 15-17

There is no space here to pursue the thread through the rest of Acts in detail. As Acts continues, so does the Gentile mission and the progress of the new faith toward the heart of the Roman Empire. The new Christians still have to deal in very concrete ways with existing cultural tensions and the power of Roman authority. Luke makes clear in various places that the church itself in Acts is only beginning to figure out the practical implications of Pentecost. Life is still messy, and prejudices and patterns of power do not shift overnight.[35] However, the key ethnic and cultural divides have in principle fallen. As David Seccombe summarizes,

> In three decades from A.D. 30 to 60, the notion of "the people of God" was transformed within early Christianity from a community largely limited to the racial descendents of the patriarch Jacob, with its focal point the God of Abraham and the land of Israel, to a multi-

racial world fellowship also focused on the God of Abraham, but also on the Messiah Jesus enthroned as King at his right hand. As a result of this change world history turned into a radically new direction.[36]

Pentecost thus began a trajectory that continued throughout Luke's account of the early church. It did not stop there.

SOME IMPLICATIONS OF BEING CHRISTIAN

In his work on the history of the worldwide Christian church, Andrew Walls observes a contrast between Islam and Christianity in terms of the dynamics of their growth. Islam, he notes, "can point to a steady geographical progression from its birthplace and from its earliest years" and during this period "has not had many territorial losses to record."[37] It also carries substantial fixed cultural content tied to the Qur'an in heaven, Mecca on earth, and Arabic as the perfect medium for its message. Christianity, on the other hand, has undergone a series of cultural translations, moving into new and marginal cultural territories and dying away in areas that were once its heartlands. This continuous movement into new cultural settings is not accidental: "For Christians . . . the divine Word is translatable, infinitely translatable. The very words of Christ himself were transmitted in translated form in the earliest documents we have, a fact surely inseparable from the conviction that in Christ, God's own self was translated into human form."[38]

The early church, as we have seen, was characterized by a series of negotiations of cultural boundaries. By the time Jerusalem fell, what Walls refers to as the "Hellenistic-Roman" model of Christianity was well established, but a few centuries later the Roman world was in turn to face its terminal crisis, at which time the heartlands of Christianity moved further north into northern Europe. Early flowerings of Christian faith in Africa and Asia also faded as the centuries passed, creating the temporary illusion that Christianity was essentially a Western or even a European religion. Following the shift in the center of gravity from Europe to North America, the most spectacular recent growth has been back in Africa and Asia and in Latin America. Walls notes that "in the year 1800 well over 90 percent of the world's professing Christians lived in Europe or North America. Today, something like 60 percent of them live in Africa, Asia, Latin America or the Pacific, and that proportion is rising year by year."[39] Over the past century alone, Walls points out, the number of professing Christians in Africa has risen from around 10 million to more than 300 million, renewing an ancient heritage of African Christian faith that began in Acts 8.[40] The list of nations with the highest numbers of Christians prominently includes Mexico, Brazil, Nigeria, and the Philippines.[41] As was noted in the prologue, the typical Christian, if there is such a thing, is not white and English-speaking, and we can no longer think of the history of Christianity as a history of the Western church plus missions.

The key point here, however, is not simply one of numerical shift, but one of cultural shift. These changes in the center of gravity of the Christian world have been inseparable from the development of new expressions of Christian faith and practice woven into new cultural settings. Theological emphases, specific worship practices, hierarchies of sin and virtue, and forms of church organization have emerged out of the church taking root in particular cultural locations (this of course includes the cultural specifics of Western Christianity).[42] There has been a constant process of retranslation. There have inevitably been episodes both of capitulation to aspects of local culture that in the long haul turn out to be in tension with the kingdom of God and of unjustified imposition of alien cultural practices in new settings in the name of Christian faith. Nevertheless, however often we have erred by enthroning some aspect of our own or another's culture, intercultural learning remains essential to the identity and history of Christianity, not merely something that resides at its fringes.

That this is so has to do with what it means to be part of the church. Walls turns to Paul's description of the reconciliation that flows from the gospel of Christ in Ephesians 2. Now that "foreigners to the convenants," those who were "far away," have been "brought near by the blood of Christ," the former "dividing wall of hostility" is removed, creating "one new humanity" (Ephesians 2:11-16). Believers, whatever their origins, are now "no longer foreigners and strangers" to one another (2:19). Instead, Paul pictures believers as the various stones being used to build a new temple: "you too are being built together to become a dwelling in which God lives through his Spirit" (2:22). No one group can claim to be the whole building; the temple emerges as we are "joined together." The church must be one since Christ is one, affirming in his humanity all of humanity in all of its cultural diversity. Believers of different cultural backgrounds and practices are therefore to become (in another of Paul's metaphors, developed in Ephesians 4) parts of a single body. It is not my culture or someone else's that provides the basic framework — the cornerstone and head are Christ, not some particular cultural group of Christians. Each part of the body retains its difference, yet needs the others for maturity:

> Remember that at that time you were separate from Christ, excluded from citizenship in Israel and foreigners to the covenants of the promise, without hope and without God in the world. But now in Christ Jesus you who once were far away have been brought near by the blood of Christ. For he himself is our peace, who has made the two one and has destroyed the barrier, the dividing wall of hostility, by setting aside in his flesh the law with its commands and regulations. His purpose was to create in himself one new humanity out of the two, thus making peace, and in one body to reconcile both of them to God through the cross, by which he put to death their hostility.
>
> EPHESIANS 2:12-16

> The Ephesian metaphors of the temple and of the body show each of the culture-specific segments as necessary to the body but as incomplete in itself. Only in Christ does completion, fullness, dwell. And Christ's completion, as we have seen, comes from all humanity, from the translation of the life of Jesus into the lifeways of all the world's cultures and subcultures through history. None of us can reach Christ's completeness on our own. We need each other's vision to correct, enlarge, and focus our own; only together are we complete in Christ.[43]

What does this mean practically for those who profess Christian faith? It means first that on theological grounds, as well as because of the simple facts regarding how the worldwide church is made up, to profess Christian faith implies a willingness to grow together with fellow believers whose ethnicities, languages, and cultures are different from my own. To pretend otherwise would be like professing to be an ardent Chicago Bulls fan but refusing to take any interest in basketball (you can substitute your own culturally fitting simile). To be Christian is to lay down one's claim to be whole, self-sufficient, and complete in oneself, the standard by which others should be measured. To be Christian is to imitate Christ's open-armed embrace of Jew and Gentile, male and female, slave and free, barbarian, Scythian, African, European, Latino, Asian, and so on (Colossians 3:11; Galatians 3:28). To be Christian is, furthermore, not to reserve for oneself the role of host, the one who sets the table, but to learn to see Christ in others, to receive correction from them, to be joined to them, to learn from the stranger.[44]

> Consequently, you are no longer foreigners and strangers, but fellow citizens with God's people and also members of his household, built on the foundation of the apostles and prophets, with Christ Jesus himself as the chief cornerstone. In him the whole building is joined together and rises to become a holy temple in the Lord. And in him you too are being built together to become a dwelling in which God lives by his Spirit.
>
> EPHESIANS 2:19-22

The book that concludes the New Testament, Revelation, is still echoing the trajectory of Pentecost. A recurring motif mentions those of every tribe, language, people, and nation who are caught up in the unfolding drama of redemption. There is no romantic celebration of the exotic here: good and evil, salvation and suffering are writ large across the landscape. What is clear, however, is that the line demarcating good and evil is not drawn between cultures, races, or nations.[45] There are those from *every* people, tribe, language, and nation, we are told, who cause suffering, oppress others, reject repentance, and bow before the beast (Revelation 11:9; 13:7; 17:15). Sin and deception know no political, ethnic, linguistic, or geographical boundaries. In the same tumult of events, however, we find those from *every* people, tribe, language, and nation who stand in white robes before the Lamb with palm branches in their hands, joined together in peace, purity, and thankfulness for salvation (Revelation 5:9; 7:9; 10:11; 14:6). Salvation, truth, and wholeness are similarly disdainful of national and cultural borders. None are included because their ethnic or cultural identity makes them superior; none are excluded because their ethnic or cultural identity makes them inferior.

There is, moreover, no indication that people's different identities are simply left behind. Those drawn from all the nations, people groups, and language groups are made pure, refined, and joined in harmony. No doubt, in each case there must be pruning, repentance, giving up of habits and practices that fail the test of wholeness. But there is no sign of everyone being melted down into uniformity (let alone remade in the image of one of the source cultures). Continuing the trajectory set at Pentecost, the miracle is not that all are given the same language, but that they become able to hear one another; it is not that they become one another, but that they love one another. Revelation offers us a final vision of people of every cultural origin drawn together through shared love of God and love of each other as themselves. To be Christian is to hope for this, and to actively seek the realization of that hope. Such seeking cannot take place without learning from the stranger.

> After this I looked, and there before me was a great multitude that no one could count, from every nation, tribe, people and language, standing before the throne and in front of the Lamb. They were wearing white robes and were holding palm branches in their hands.
>
> **REVELATION 7:9**

CHOOSING THE JOURNEY

At the beginning of this book I outlined the need for a framework for thinking in Christian terms about learning other languages and cultures in a way that takes seriously learning from the stranger. I have spent seven chapters endeavoring to lay out such a framework and to ground it theologically. I began with Abraham's discovery that the pagan ruler whom he feared could be spoken to by God and could be the means by which Abraham's fears and failures were challenged. At the heart of the book we considered how Jesus challenged a teacher of the law to learn how to obey the Scriptures from an outsider, a Samaritan. Finally, the last chapter described the birth of the early church at Pentecost and the progressive overcoming of cultural boundaries that resulted from that initial impetus and empowerment, ending at a point yet before us when those of every people, nation, tribe, and tongue stand whole, shoulder to shoulder. I suggest that these episodes, while not the only ones that could be consulted, offer essential building materials for a Christian approach to intercultural learning.

Having closed the last chapter on a somewhat cosmic note, I want to look back down to earth one more time before leaving you in peace. It has always been notoriously possible to embrace high-minded principles while failing the test of daily reality. More specifically, it has always been notoriously possible to love humankind with fervent and noble affection while failing the more difficult, messy, and tedious task of genuinely caring for the concrete person under our nose. Loving my neighbor as myself is, and should be, a challenging, disquieting, inspiring idea. It is often harder to embrace the small, slow gains, discouraging setbacks, and real frustrations of actually mastering another language, learning to function in another cultural setting, and patiently listening to actual other people (especially if I don't find them immediately insightful, or if I feel threatened by what they have to say). On the ground, it is plain hard work.

Partly as a result of working on this book, I have myself been challenged to respond afresh and concretely to the call to love the stranger, even though I have already learned and taught several languages and have long been involved in intercultural learning in various settings. With a few other members of my church, I recently began volunteering as a tutor, teaching English to a refugee family from Burundi, newly arrived in Grand Rapids and learning to function in the United States. Once or twice a week I meet with the family at their house to practice speaking and reading, beginning at the very beginning. Progress is slow, and at the moment there is very little we can say to one another. I have heard some of the family's story through an interpreter, but when we meet for language practice we are for the present stuck at the level of greetings, numbers, and household objects. The family members are dutiful students, eager to learn and at times impatient at the limits of what they can communicate. During my visits, I ask them to tell me how to say in Kirundi some of the things that they are learning in English. At those moments, when they are briefly restored to competence, and it is my turn to become the feeble learner, their smiles broaden and become more relaxed, more joyful, while I, holder of graduate degrees in language education though I may be, am reduced once more to the childlike position of struggling to retain unfamiliar sounds in my short-term memory for long enough to massacre them as I try to say them back. In this way, week by week we give small gifts to one another. It is unglamorous; it will take a great deal of time; it involves driving across town in the snow when I have other things to be doing. And it is a way of seeking to love the stranger. It is part of my individual response to working on this book.

What will your response to reading the book be? I hope that the book has been informative, but I confess that I am after more. I have tried to touch your ideals, but I also hope that those ideals will motivate your actions, your small, unglamorous, painstaking actions that may one day have added up to loving your neighbor. What opportunities are in your life? Are there classes you need to take, or work at more diligently, or with a different spirit? Are there individuals around you whose voice you have not taken the time to hear? Are there people in your vicinity whom you could serve, and from whom you could learn? Are there issues in your community which could use your advocacy? Where could you begin, or what could you strengthen? What choices need to be made?

The novel *Vipers' Tangle* by the French Nobel laureate François Mauriac portrays a cantankerous elderly businessman reflecting back on his life, and on how his past choices have shaped his present. "The horror of old age," he laments, "is that it is the sum-total of a life — a sum-total of which one cannot change a figure. I have spent sixty years creating this old man dying of hatred. I am what I am. I should have become somebody else."[1] As he begins to realize how he has allowed himself to be formed primarily by the love of money and the desire for petty revenge, he looks back with regret, not at any great crime or outstanding act of evil, but at a lifelong failure to get beyond appearances:

> It had not been enough for me, throughout half a century, to recognize nothing in myself except that which was not I. I had done the same thing in the case of other people. Those miserable greeds visible in my children's faces had fascinated me. Robert's stupidity had been what struck me about him, and I had confined myself to that superficial feature. Never had the appearance of other people presented itself to me as something that must be broken through, something that must be penetrated, before one could reach them.

Now he feels that his opportunity has passed, that the time in which he could have made formative choices lies long behind him:

> Those whom I should have loved are dead. Dead are those who might have loved me. As for the survivors, I no longer have the time, or the strength, to set out on a voyage towards them, to discover them. There is nothing in me, down to my voice, my gestures, my laugh, which does not belong to the monster whom I set up against the world, and to whom I gave my name.[2]

He discovers almost too late that what makes him a "monster" is that he has lived a life closed up within his own horizons, missing the opportunity to genuinely love and be loved by being too preoccupied with judgmental perceptions of those who have shared his world. His life has now taken on a shape made up of the concrete choices he has made, choices not to learn, not to engage.

Almost at his deathbed, he discovers that while he cannot change himself, there is still grace, even for him, that in "Someone in Whom we are all one" can be found the possibility of turning away from self-absorption. "To get beyond the absurdities, the failings, and above all the stupidity of people," he realizes, "one must possess a secret of love which the world has forgotten."[3] He discovers this secret, finding his halting way to Christian faith, only in his final days. Those of us who profess that faith and still have longer lives before us face the same choices, choices that will shape the selves that we become. Will we set ourselves up against the world and recognize nothing outside our own horizons, or will we walk in the way of Christ, the "Someone in Whom we are all one," and learn to love? May we receive the grace to choose well.

Endnotes

Notes to the Prologue

1. I am grateful to the school for permission to share this story.

2. Philip Jenkins, *The New Faces of Christianity: Believing the Bible in the Global South* (New York: Oxford University Press, 2006), p. 9.

3. Andrew F. Walls, "Eusebius Tries Again: The Task of Reconceiving and Revisioning the Study of Christian History," in *Enlarging the Story: Perspectives on Writing World Christian History,* ed. Wilbert R. Shenk (Maryknoll, N.Y.: Orbis Books, 2002), p. 1.

4. See, e.g., Sherwood G. Lingenfelter and Marvin K. Mayers, *Ministering Cross-Culturally: An Incarnational Model for Personal Relationships,* 2d ed. (Grand Rapids: Baker Academic, 2003); Duane Elmer, *Cross-Cultural Servanthood: Serving the World in Christlike Humility* (Downers Grove, Ill.: InterVarsity Press, 2006).

5. See Roger E. Axtell, *Gestures: The Do's and Taboos of Body Language Around the World,* rev. ed. (New York: John Wiley & Sons, 1998), p. 26.

6. Anyone wishing to chart my likely cultural peculiarities can consult Kate Fox, *Watching the English: The Hidden Rules of English Behavior* (London: Hodder & Stoughton, 2004).

7. As Bartholomew and Goheen comment, "Many of us have read the Bible as if it were merely a mosaic of little bits — theological bits, moral bits, historical-critical bits, sermon bits, devotional bits. But when we read the Bible in such a fragmented way, we ignore its divine author's intention to shape our lives through its story. All human communities live out of some story that provides a context for understanding the meaning of history and gives shape and direction to their lives. If we allow the Bible to become fragmented, it is in danger of being absorbed into whatever *other* story is shaping our culture, and it will cease to shape our lives as it should." Craig G. Bartholomew and Michael W. Goheen, *The Drama of Scrip-*

153

ture: Finding our Place in the Biblical Story (Grand Rapids: Baker Academic, 2004), p. 12.

8. The full quotation from Paul refers to Abraham as "the father of all who believe but have not been circumcised, in order that righteousness might be credited to them" — this itself is an example of a broadening of ethnic horizons by focusing on the salvation of non-Jews through faith; see further Chapter 7 below.

Notes to Chapter 1

1. "Abimelek" may be a title, like "Pharaoh," rather than a personal name; see John T. Willis, *Genesis* (Austin: Sweet, 1979), p. 273. In the similar story in Genesis 12, Sarah's beauty is given as the motive; here no motive is mentioned. Matthews suggests that, given Sarah's advanced age at this point in the narrative, economic motives may have been in play this time around — the formation of an economic alliance through marriage. Such motives would help explain Abimelek's lack of haste to consummate his new union. This may be another of a series of pointed dissimilarities to previous experiences that highlight the mistaken nature of Abraham's experience-based assumptions about what will happen, and may also cast Abraham's anxieties in an even poorer light if Abimelek intended mutual advantage. See Kenneth A. Matthews, *Genesis 11:27-50:26*, New American Commentary, vol. 1B (Nashville: Broadman & Holman, 2005), pp. 251-52; Nahum M. Sarna, *Genesis*, The JPS Torah Commentary (Philadelphia: Jewish Publication Society, 1989), p. 141. I have accordingly amended this section from an earlier version of this chapter, published as David I. Smith, "How Not to Bless the Nations," *Perspectives* (December 2005): 6-11.

2. As Branch notes, in Genesis the dreams of those both inside and outside the covenant fall under God's sovereignty; see Robin Gallagher Branch, "Genesis 20: A Literary Template for the Prophetic Tradition," *In die Skriftig* 38, no. 2 (2004): 217-34, at p. 223; this forms an interesting point of connection with Acts 10, discussed in Chapter 7 below.

3. Von Rad comments: "the personal blamelessness of the heathen king is delineated by the narrator to the profound humiliation of Abraham . . . it is humiliating for Abraham to have to be surpassed by the heathen in the fear of God." See Gerhard von Rad, *Genesis: A Commentary*, trans. John H. Marks (London: SCM Press, 1961), pp. 223-24. While some commentators emphasize the implication in God's comments that Abimelek would have gone on to sin if God had not restrained him (e.g., Branch, "Genesis 20," pp. 219-21), it distorts the story to see Abimelek's *potential* fault as a focal issue, rather than Abraham's *actual* faults. As Westermann notes, the acquittal of Abimelek in the story (vv. 6-7) is not balanced by an acquittal of Abraham; see Claus Westermann, *Genesis: A Practical Commentary*, trans. David E. Green (Grand Rapids: Eerdmans, 1987), p. 150. Hamilton notes that in 2 Chronicles 35:22 the godly king Josiah dies for refusing to listen to what

God said through the mouth of Pharaoh Neco; see Victor P. Hamilton, *The Book of Genesis Chapters 18-50*, New International Commentary on the Old Testament (Grand Rapids: Eerdmans, 1995), p. 61.

4. Hamilton points out that Genesis 19 and 20 both center on the behavior of a man who is an alien, and that Abraham uses of himself in verse 13 the verb "wander," used elsewhere to mean traveling "hopelessly and aimlessly, often in a hostile environment" (Hamilton, *Book of Genesis*, pp. 58, 68). On Abraham's reference to "wandering," see also J. Gerald Janzen, *Genesis 12–50: Abraham and All the Families of the Earth*, International Theological Commentary (Grand Rapids: Eerdmans, 1993), p. 70.

5. Matthews, *Genesis*, p. 251.

6. Janzen, *Genesis 12–50*, pp. 68-69.

7. See Hamilton, *The Book of Genesis*, p. 61. The wording of Abimelek's plea may imply that he regards not only himself but also his nation as righteous. Abimelek later asks Abraham what he has done to "us" and refers to effects on "me and my kingdom." The judgment of infertility likewise extends the threat of death from Abimelek individually out to his whole realm (Matthews, *Genesis*, p. 259). See also Robert D. Sacks, *A Commentary on the Book of Genesis*, Ancient Near Eastern Texts and Studies, vol. 6 (Lewiston, N.Y.: Edwin Mellen Press, 1990), pp. 141-44.

8. Assyrian laws from the second millennium B.C. that show some parallels with this story indicate that for Abimelek to take Sarah to his palace knowing she was married would have been a crime even without sexual contact; the phrase "a great sin" (v. 9) also reflects ancient Near Eastern legal terminology applied to adultery. Abimelek's insistence that he did not know she was married, and his moves to compensate financially for the inadvertent error, seem broadly consistent with this legal background and imply an image of Abimelek as law-abiding. See Umberto Cassuto, *A Commentary on the Book of Genesis*, vol. 2, trans. J. Abrahams (Jerusalem: Magnes Press, 1964), pp. 357-58; Moshe Weinfeld, "Sara and Abimelech (Genesis 20) Against the Background of an Assyrian Law and the Genesis Apocryphon," in *Mélanges Bibliques et Orientaux en L'honneur de M. Matthias Delcor* (Kevelaer, West Germany: Butzon und Bercker, 1985), pp. 431-36; Sarna, *Genesis*, p. 143.

9. Martin Kessler and Karel Deurloo, *A Commentary on Genesis: The Book of Beginnings* (New York: Paulist Press, 2004), p. 124.

10. The importance of not "understanding" too quickly is discussed further in Chapter 6.

11. Paul Borgman, *Genesis: The Story We Haven't Heard* (Downers Grove, Ill.: InterVarsity Press, 2001), pp. 47-48.

12. The connection back to Abraham's call to be a blessing to the "peoples" in Genesis 12 is visible in Abimelek's appeal to God not to destroy "an innocent people" in vv. 4-5. See Matthews, *Genesis*, p. 253.

Notes to Chapter 2

1. Ralph Linton, from *The Study of Man* (1936), cited in Paul Marshall, "Living with Our Differences: Values and Beliefs in a Pluralist Society," paper presented at the EurECA Conference, St. Chrischona, Switzerland, May 9, 1994.

2. Bruce Olson, *Bruchko* (Chichester: New Wine Press, 1978), p. 50.

3. Lindy Scott, "North American Christians and the Latin American Church: Lessons from South of the Border," *Journal of Christianity and Foreign Languages* 3 (2002): 48-75, at p. 50.

4. A recent manual bringing together worship music from around the world is C. Michael Hawn, *Gather into One: Praying and Singing Globally* (Grand Rapids: Eerdmans, 2003).

5. Bert H. Hodges, "Perception Is Relative and Veridical: Biblical and Ecological Perspectives on Knowing and Doing the Truth," in *The Reality of Christian Learning*, ed. Harold Heie and David L. Wolfe (Grand Rapids: Eerdmans, 1987), pp. 104-5.

6. See Miguel A. de la Torre, *Reading the Bible from the Margins* (Maryknoll, N.Y.: Orbis Books, 2003), pp. 104-35.

7. Jacques Ellul, *The Humiliation of the Word* (Grand Rapids: Eerdmans, 1985), pp. 17-18.

8. Muriel Saville-Troike, "Cultural Maintenance and 'Vanishing' Languages," in *Text and Context: Cross-Disciplinary Perspectives on Language Study*, ed. Claire Kramsch and Sally McConnell-Ginet (Lexington, Mass.: D. C. Heath & Co., 1992), p. 151.

9. A reader of a draft of this chapter related the following anecdote: "We were reminded of our encounter with Polish drunks on a bus one morning. We were out early one morning in the city of Torun and the only two people on the bus when two young men got on who were stumbling drunk. Knowing the boorish behavior of English and American drunks, our apprehension must have shown on our faces. However these two actually apologized for being drunk! [My husband] was able to catch most of the explanation that they'd just finished their mandatory two years of military service the night before and had been out celebrating. Polish culture is very polite, but we were astounded that even drunks were polite there!" Lynda Warner, personal communication.

10. Heath offers the following summary of the ethnographic and psychological findings: "There is overwhelming historical and cross-cultural evidence that people learn not only how to drink but how to be affected by drink through a process of socialization. . . . Numerous experiments conducted under strictly controlled conditions (double-blind, with placebos) on a wide range of subjects and in different cultures have demonstrated that both mood and actions are affected far more by what people think they have drunk than by what they have actually drunk. . . . In simple terms, this means that people who expect drinking to result in violence become aggressive; those who expect it to make them feel sexy be-

come amorous; those who view it as disinhibiting are demonstrative. If behavior reflects expectations, then a society gets the drunks it deserves." Dwight B. Heath, "Cultural Variations Among Drinking Patterns," in *Drinking Patterns and Their Consequences,* ed. Marcus Grant and Jorge Litvak (Washington: Taylor & Francis, 1998), p. 115. The classic study of global variability in drunken behavior is Craig MacAndrew and Robert B. Edgerton, *Drunken Comportment: A Social Explanation* (Chicago: Aldine, 1969). For a recent review of research, see http://www.sirc.org/publik/drinking4.html.

11. The following exercise was suggested to me by similar exercises used by Richard Slimbach of Azusa Pacific University.

12. I owe the following description entirely to my colleague Larry Herzberg.

Notes to Chapter 3

1. Saint Augustine, *Confessions,* trans. Henry Chadwick (New York: Oxford University Press, 1991), p. 7. Augustine's account actually begins further back still, with the mystery of God and creation; infancy is, however, where the young Augustine comes explicitly onto the stage.

2. Augustine, *Confessions,* pp. 7-8.

3. As Bakhtin points out, none of us is "the first speaker, the one who disturbs the eternal silence of the universe" — when we speak we use words provided by others. Our words are "filled with echoes" of the ways that others have used them — they "taste" of their previous contexts, so that "our speech . . . is filled with others' words, varying degrees of otherness or varying degrees of 'our-own-ness.'" Mikhail M. Bakhtin, *Speech Genres and Other Late Essays,* trans. V. W. McGee (Austin: University of Texas Press, 1986), pp. 69, 88-89.

4. A more detailed description of the experiments described here, together with references to the primary research reports, can be found in the first two chapters of Gerry T. M. Altmann, *The Ascent of Babel: An Exploration of Language, Mind, and Understanding* (New York: Oxford University Press, 1997).

5. These differences even appear in the ways in which we pronounce individual words. For instance, following different stress patterns in different varieties of English, people say *con*troversy or con*tro*versy, *re*search or re*search,* A*ug*ustine or Au*gus*tine.

6. There are of course instances that do not quite fit this pattern, such as children born to parents who communicate in sign language; they remain, however, exceptions to the common situation.

7. Bakhtin, *Speech Genres,* p. 89.

8. Richard E. Nisbett, *The Geography of Thought: How Asians and Westerners Think Differently . . . and Why* (New York: The Free Press, 2003), p. 150.

9. Nisbett, *Geography of Thought.* For the particular examples that follow, see pp. 59, 87, 127.

10. Nisbett, *Geography of Thought*, p. 59.

11. Rick Kirkman and Jeremy Scott, "Baby Blues," *Grand Rapids Press*, Sept. 20, 2007, p. B11.

12. Our various culturally located responses to creation are answerable to reality, but do not exhaustively contain reality. A culture is a particular way of living in and responding to a real world (Algerians do not develop rituals around seal hunting) even as it represents that world in partial and sometimes dysfunctional ways. See further James K. A. Smith, *The Fall of Interpretation: Philosophical Foundations for a Creational Hermeneutic* (Downers Grove, Ill.: InterVarsity Press, 2000).

13. See, e.g., Michael Newton, *Savage Girls and Wild Boys: A History of Feral Children* (New York: Thomas Dunne Books, 2003).

14. Helen Keller, *The World I Live In*, cited in William J. Vande Kopple, "Toward a Christian View of Language," in *Contemporary Literary Theory: A Christian Appraisal*, ed. Clarence Walhout and Leland Ryken (Grand Rapids: Eerdmans, 1991), p. 213.

15. As Augustine realized: "I gradually gathered the meaning of words, occurring in their places in different sentences and frequently heard, and already I learnt to articulate my wishes by training my mouth to use these signs. In this way I communicated the signs of my wishes to those around me, and entered more deeply into the stormy society of human life. I was dependent on the authority of my parents and the direction of adult people. . . . I learnt Latin. . . . My own heart constrained me to bring its concepts to birth, which I could not have done unless I had learnt some words." Augustine, *Confessions*, pp. 11, 17.

16. This is not an unfair parallel, for the ears of different creatures pick up different sounds, and human hearers lose (at least until relearning occurs) the ability, present at birth, to discriminate certain linguistic sounds if the distinctions that they represent are not present in the culture in which socialization takes place. Our ears are not simply mirrors for the auditory world.

17. As Peter Enns writes, "This is what it means for God to speak at a certain time and place — he enters *their* world. He speaks and acts in ways that make sense to *them*. This is surely what it means for God to reveal himself to people — he accommodates, condescends, meets them where they are. The phrase *word of God* does not imply disconnectedness to its environment. In fact, if we can learn a lesson from the incarnation of God in Christ, it demands the exact opposite. . . . We must resist the notion that for God to enculturate himself is somehow beneath him. This is precisely how he shows his love to the world he has made." Peter Enns, *Inspiration and Incarnation: Evangelicals and the Problem of the Old Testament* (Grand Rapids: Baker Academic, 2005), p. 56.

18. Vande Kopple, "Christian View," p. 212. There is a longstanding debate concerning the degree to which and the manner in which language may be innate. Regardless of the particularities of that debate, it is clear that whatever innate capacities for language we have, these are activated through interaction with

other speakers of a particular language, whose particular words and speech patterns belong to a particular culture.

19. For fuller discussion of what this realization implies for hermeneutics, as well as of the tensions in Augustine's views, see Smith, *The Fall of Interpretation.*

20. Charles T. Mathewes, "Book One: The Presumptuousness of Autobiography and the Paradoxes of Beginning," in *A Reader's Companion to Augustine's Confessions,* ed. Kim Paffenroth and Robert P. Kennedy (Louisville: Westminster John Knox Press, 2003), pp. 7-23. As McFarland puts it, "our life [as] persons requires a prior act of compassion in which another person treats us as persons." See Ian A. McFarland, "Who Is My Neighbor? The Good Samaritan as a Source for Theological Anthropology," *Modern Theology* 17, no. 1 (2001): 63.

21. Paulo Freire, *Pedagogy of the Oppressed* (New York: Continuum, 2000).

22. See, e.g., Ron Ritchhart, *Intellectual Character: What It Is, Why It Matters, and How to Get It* (San Francisco: Jossey-Bass, 2004), pp. 12-13.

23. Charles Marsh, *The Beloved Community: How Faith Shapes Social Justice from the Civil Rights Movement to Today* (New York: Basic Books, 2005), p. 57.

24. Augustine, *Confessions,* p. 18.

25. James H. Olthuis, "Be(com)ing: Humankind as Gift and Call," *Philosophia Reformata* 58 (1993): 153-72.

26. J. Richard Middleton, *The Liberating Image: The Imago Dei in Genesis 1* (Grand Rapids: Brazos, 2005), p. 252.

27. Middleton, *Liberating Image,* p. 121.

28. It is also harder than it seems. It is easy enough to say that all cultures are fine, but as soon as we run into, say, a movie or piece of music that grates on our cultural sensibilities, or a behavior that strikes us as bizarre, or a belief that seems to us to be objectionable or harmful, our response is almost guaranteed to include an element of judgment that our own position is in some sense "better." It is easiest to be relativists concerning aspects of culture that are distant and do not affect us, or that do not challenge or disturb us.

29. Commenting on this passage, N. T. Wright writes: "There is no sphere of existence over which Jesus is not sovereign, in virtue of his role both in creation ([Col.] 1:16-17) and in reconciliation (1:18-20). There can be no dualistic division between some areas which he rules and others which he does not. . . . The task of evangelism is therefore best understood as the proclamation that Jesus is already Lord, that in him God's new creation has broken into history, and that all people are therefore summoned to submit to him in love, worship, and obedience. The logic of this message requires that those who announce it should be seeking to bring Christ's Lordship to bear on every area of human and worldly existence. Christians must work to help create conditions in which human beings, and the whole created world, can live as God always intended." N. T. Wright, *Colossians and Philemon,* Tyndale New Testament Commentaries (Leicester: InterVarsity Press, 1986), pp. 79-80.

Notes to Chapter 4

1. Regarding the reformulation of the scribe's initial question, see Charles H. Talbert, *Reading Luke: A Literary and Theological Commentary on the Third Gospel* (New York: Crossroad, 1982), p. 121: "Since it is two Jews talking and since it was assumed by Jews that the people of God would inherit the New Age, the import of the question is clear. The lawyer is asking what he as an individual should do to guarantee his place in the people of God who would inherit eternal life: 'What do I do to belong to God's people?' Moreover, when the lawyer asks, 'Who is my neighbor?' he is wanting to know how he can spot others who belong to God's covenant people. The Jews interpreted 'neighbor' in terms of members of the same people or religious community, that is, fellow Jews. . . . Jews generally excluded Samaritans and foreigners from the category of neighbor." Talbert also (p. 122) indicates the conventional nature of the response to the initial question — these two commands were combined in Jewish thought before Jesus.

2. See Kenneth E. Bailey, *Poet and Peasant and Through Peasant Eyes: A Literary-Cultural Approach to the Parables in Luke* (Grand Rapids: Eerdmans, 1983), pp. 33-34.

3. See N. T. Wright, *Jesus and the Victory of God* (London: SPCK, 1996), pp. 305-7.

4. See Talbert, *Reading Luke*, pp. 121-22; also Darrell L. Bock, *Luke Volume 2: 9:51–24:53*, Baker Exegetical Commentary on the New Testament (Grand Rapids: Baker Books, 1996), p. 1023.

5. See Bailey, *Poet and Peasant*, pp. 39-40. Hendrickx points out that in the occupied conditions of Israel in the first century A.D. it could not be assumed that those dwelling among the people of Israel qualified as neighbors even in the extended sense of foreigners who had joined themselves religiously to Israel. See Herman Hendrickx, *The Third Gospel for the Third World, Volume Three — A Travel Narrative I (Luke 9:51–13:21)* (Quezon City, Philippines: Claretian Publications, 2000), p. 62.

6. Bock, *Luke*, pp. 1026-27. As Búason notes, of the three questions in the exchange, this is the only non-rhetorical question, the only question with a contested answer. See Kristján Búason, "The Good Samaritan, Luke 10:25-37: One Text, Three Methods," in *Luke-Acts: Scandinavian Perspectives*, ed. Petri Luomanen (Helsinki: The Finnish Exegetical Society; Göttingen: Vandenhoek & Ruprecht, 1991), pp. 1-35, at pp. 10, 12.

7. See John Nolland, *Luke 9:21–18:34*, Word Biblical Commentary, vol. 35B (Dallas: Word Books, 1993), p. 593.

8. The fact that several details of the parable echo and invoke the account from 2 Chronicles 28, in which an Israelite army from the Northern capital of Samaria first massacres Judean forces and then, under the rebuke of a prophet, tends the wounded in the ways described, may be a subtle acknowledgment of (and refusal to condone) a history of bloodshed between North and South going

even further back than the origins of the Samaritans as a distinct people. Jesus' reworking of motifs from this earlier mercy story omits both the context of war and the accusation of defective following of God that legitimated war (2 Chronicles 28:6); the Samaritan and the Jews become in Jesus' tale merely travelers along the same road. Jesus may be seeking to undermine present hostility by alluding to the fact that the last mention of Samaria in the Old Testament before the exile describes an act of mercy in obedient response to the word of God; see Michael P. Knowles, "What Was the Victim Wearing? Literary, Economic and Social Contexts for the Parable of the Good Samaritan," *Biblical Interpretation* 12, no. 2 (2004): 145-74; although the differences in connotation between (pre-exilic) Samarian and (post-exilic) Samaritan suggest some caution is needed on this point. It is also interesting that the account in 2 Chronicles 28 appears to model the apostasy of Judah after that of Israel just after the post-Solomon schism, reversing the relationship of North and South. At the schism the righteous left the North and came to Judah, and Judah heeded the word of a prophet against attacking the sister kingdom (2 Chronicles 11:1-4); now it is Judah that has sunk into apostasy and the North that is responsive to prophetic correction. These reversals are elaborated in more detail in Raymond B. Dillard, *2 Chronicles,* Word Biblical Commentary (Waco: Word Books, 1987), pp. 219-21; and they make the Chronicles episode a fitting backdrop to the pride-undermining reversals of Jesus' parable.

9. Many commentators argue that the traveler is assumed in the story to be a Jew, because of his journey starting in Jerusalem and because of the implied contrast with the Samaritan. Neither argument is, however, decisive. Here I follow Esler, who argues that Jesus is already deliberately complicating the scribe's initial question by withholding information about the victim's ethnicity; the victim could well be Jewish, but Jesus is already refusing to play by the scribe's rules — he implies that we do not need to know. The Samaritan, when he arrives on the scene, does not act as if the question of the victim's ethnicity is relevant to his decisions. See Philip F. Esler, "Jesus and the Reduction of Intergroup Conflict: The Parable of the Good Samaritan in the Light of Social Identity Theory," *Biblical Interpretation* 8, no. 4 (2000): 325-57, especially pp. 337-41. See also Bailey, *Poet and Peasant,* pp. 42-43.

10. Esler, "Intergroup Conflict," p. 341. Bailey (*Poet and Peasant,* p. 43) notes that the priest, given his social status, was highly likely to be riding, and so had the same resources for aiding the victim as the Samaritan.

11. Esler, "Intergroup Conflict," pp. 338-41. Bauckham argues for ritual uncleanness as a motivation; see Richard Bauckham, "The Scrupulous Priest and the Good Samaritan: Jesus' Parabolic Interpretation of the Law of Moses," *New Testament Studies* 44 (1998): 475-89. Esler points out that the uncertain ethnic identity complicates this, since the prohibitions on a priest touching a corpse in Leviticus 21:1-4 may only apply to an Israelite corpse.

12. The discussion between Jesus and the scribe opened with a combination of two commandments from the Old Testament, one concerned with loving

God and one concerned with loving one's neighbor. Some commentators have suggested that the parable of the "good Samaritan" deals with the second of these, and that the story about Martha and Mary and the one thing needful is placed immediately after it by Luke as matching commentary on the first (see, e.g., Nolland, *Luke*). Whatever the merits of this suggestion at the level of Luke's larger narrative structure, in terms of his account of Jesus' exchange with the scribe (the Martha/ Mary episode is preceded by a change of location) it seems possible that the more immediate point is that loving the neighbor is inseparable from loving God. This episode differs from similar accounts in the other Gospels (Matthew 19:16-22; 22:34-40; Mark 12:28-34) in running the two commands together into a single command (cf. Luke Timothy Johnson, *The Gospel of Luke*, Sacra Pagina Series, vol. 3 [Collegeville, Minn.: The Liturgical Press, 1991], p. 174). If the priest and the Levite are coming from the temple and are indeed, as has often been suggested, motivated by desire to keep the purity laws, then part of Jesus' point in critiquing them could be that they are seeking to love God with all their might without attending to the needs of their neighbor, a position painted as untenable not only by Jesus, but by a longer prophetic tradition (see, e.g., Jeremiah 7). Given the lack of attention to motive in the story, however, this remains speculative.

13. Gourgues notes the existence of a rabbinic formula for referring to the layers of Israel society as "the priests, the Levites, and all the people," and suggests that it indicates a narrative expectation that the third traveler will be one of the common people. See Michel Gourgues, "The Priest, the Levite, and the Samaritan Revisited: A Critical Note on Luke 10:31-35," *Journal of Biblical Literature* 117, no. 4 (1998): 709-13.

14. Cited in Esler, "Intergroup Conflict," p. 330; I draw the other details in this paragraph principally from Esler and from J. Jeremias, "Σαμάρεια, Σαμαρίτης, Σαμαρῖτις," in *Theological Dictionary of the New Testament*, vol. 7, ed. Gerhard Friedrich, trans. Geoffrey W. Bromiley (Grand Rapids: Eerdmans, 1971), pp. 88-93.

15. Bock, *Luke*, p. 1033. On the other details here see also Bailey, *Poet and Peasant*.

16. Samaritans are designated foreigners in Luke 17:18, in the midst of another Lukan story that undermines Jewish antipathy toward Samaritans.

17. Bock, *Luke*, p. 1035; Anthony Lee Ash, *The Gospel According to Luke, Part II: 9:51–24:53* (Austin: Sweet Publishing Company, 1973), p. 21.

18. This apparent broadening of Leviticus 19:18 had in Jewish tradition come to be interpreted narrowly, including only foreigners who resided in Israel and were full converts to Judaism (Esler, "Intergroup Conflict," p. 336). Jesus blows open such constrictive readings.

19. As Gnanavaram puts it, Jesus confronts us with an "act of kindness which transcends the traditional barriers of culture and society." See M. Gnanavaram, "'Dalit Theology' and the Parable of the Good Samaritan," *Journal for the Study of the New Testament* 50 (1993): 59-83, at p. 73.

20. Bock, *Luke*, p. 1028.

21. Isaak describes the attitude sought by Jesus in terms of the African idea of *ubuntu* — someone with *ubuntu* is "welcoming, hospitable, warm and generous, with a servant spirit that affirms others and says 'I am because you are; you are because I am.'" Paul John Isaak, *Luke*, in *Africa Bible Commentary*, ed. Tokunboh Adeyemo (Nairobi, Kenya: WordAlive Publishers; Grand Rapids: Zondervan, 2006), p. 1225.

22. Bock, *Luke*, p. 1024.

23. Nolland argues that in his response to the question, "Who is my neighbor?" in the parable of the Samaritan, "Jesus suggests that we should answer that question from a vantage point of isolation and desperate need, and then make use of the same answer when we come at the question from a position of strength, when it is within our gift to be handing out favors, rather than receiving them." See Nolland, *Luke*, p. 597. On this reading, the import of the parable turns out to echo very closely the Golden Rule.

24. For a detailed account of the scriptural, logical, and traditional connections between the two commands, see Keith D. Stanglin, "The Historical Connection between the Golden Rule and the Second Greatest Love Commandment," *Journal of Religious Ethics* 33, no. 2 (2005): 357-71.

25. As recognized, for instance, by Augustine. See Stanglin, "Historical Connection," pp. 365-68. The argument would be: "I would like him or her to seduce me, therefore I should seduce him or her."

26. John Topel, "The Tarnished Golden Rule (Luke 6:31): The Inescapable Radicalness of Christian Ethics," *Theological Studies* 59, no. 3 (Spring 1998): 475-85, at p. 478.

27. On the relationship between the Golden Rule and the command to love enemies, see Alan Kirk, "'Love Your Enemies': The Golden Rule and Ancient Reciprocity (Luke 6:27-35)," *Journal of Biblical Literature* 122, no. 4 (2003): 667-86.

28. Amy G. Oden, ed., *And You Welcomed Me: A Sourcebook on Hospitality in Early Christianity* (Nashville: Abingdon, 2001), p. 109.

29. See Búason, "Good Samaritan," pp. 4-5, 19.

30. Cf. Robert W. Funk, "The Good Samaritan as Metaphor," *Semeia* 2 (1974): 75-84.

31. As McFarland puts it, "As it turns out, 'neighbor' is not a category that the lawyer is authorized to apply to others; instead, it takes the form of a challenge and recoils back on him as a moral agent capable either of being or of failing to be a neighbor to someone else. In this way, Jesus asks lawyer and reader alike to consider the possibility that the question of their own status as neighbors might be anthropologically prior to any reflection on the status of other people." See Ian A. McFarland, "Who Is My Neighbor? The Good Samaritan as a Source for Theological Anthropology," *Modern Theology* 17, no. 1 (2001): 57-66, at p. 60.

32. John Nolland, "The Role of Money and Possessions in the Parable of the Prodigal Son (Luke 15:11-32): A Test Case," in *Reading Luke: Interpretation, Reflection, Formation*, ed. Craig G. Bartholomew, Joel B. Green, and Anthony C.

Thiselton (Milton Keynes: Paternoster Press; Grand Rapids: Zondervan, 2005), p. 180.

33. Bock (*Luke*, p. 1033) notes that in some Jewish circles, to receive oil or wine from a Samaritan was not allowed. Cultural pride is manifested not only in the issue of whose company one is willing to keep, but perhaps still more sharply in the question: From whom is one willing to receive?

34. Esler, "Intergroup Conflict," p. 333.

35. Jeanne Stevenson Moessner, "Preaching the Good Samaritan: A Feminist Perspective," *Journal for Preachers* 9, no. 1 (1995): 21-25, at p. 21.

36. See Gnanavaram, "Dalit Theology"; Néstor O. Míguez, "La Parábola del Bueno Samaritano. Contexto, Sujeto e Interpretación," *Cuadernos de Teologia* 22 (2003): 65-78.

Notes to Chapter 5

1. Dewi Hughes, *Castrating Culture: A Christian Perspective on Ethnic Identity from the Margins* (Carlisle: Paternoster, 2000).

2. Some cultural groups have identified their own society or ethnicity with the concept of the people of God in a way that allows them to read the experiences of Old Testament Israel directly onto their own. It then becomes tempting to appeal to passages in Scripture in which Israel is warned against contamination by foreigners. In the last chapter of Nehemiah, for instance, we find a violent outburst on Nehemiah's part against those returning exiles who had married foreign women:

> the book of Moses was read aloud in the hearing of the people and there it was found written that no Ammonite or Moabite should ever be admitted into the assembly of God. . . . When the people heard this law, they excluded from Israel all who were of foreign descent. . . . In those days I [Nehemiah] saw men of Judah who had married women from Ashdod, Ammon, and Moab. Half of their children spoke the language of Ashdod or the language of one of the other peoples, and did not know how to speak the language of Judah. I rebuked them and called curses down upon them. I beat some of the men and pulled out their hair. I made them take an oath in God's name and said, "You are not to give your daughters in marriage to their sons, nor are you to take their daughters in marriage for your sons or yourselves. Was it not because of marriages such as these that Solomon king of Israel sinned?" (13:1-2, 23-26)

Such passages seem to offer fuel for theologies of apartheid and exclusion, but only if we identify Christian identity with ethnic identity. Even apart from the difficult question of how to read such passages within their Old Testament context (on the one hand, the peculiar combination of ethnicity and election found in Old Testament Israel raises a set of issues around purity that are unique to that setting; on the other, Nehemiah's is not the only voice in the Old Testament — passages such as Genesis 12, Leviticus 19, and particularly Isaiah 56 offer the possibility of critique of Nehemiah's position from within the Old Testament), such a stance is explicitly and repeatedly abandoned in the New Testament (see Chapters 4 and 7 of the present volume). Present-day Christians tempted to foreground passages in which wariness of foreigners is enjoined would do well to first meditate on the fact that unless we are direct ethnic descendents of the Israelites, we are ourselves the foreigners against which Israel was warned, now allowed into the community of faith by grace (Romans 11:17-22).

3. See Richard J. Mouw, *He Shines in All That's Fair: Culture and Common Grace* (Grand Rapids: Eerdmans, 2001).

4. John Calvin, *Institutes of the Christian Religion,* ed. John T. McNeill, trans. Ford Lewis Battles (Philadelphia: Westminster Press, 1960), 2.2.15, p. 273.

5. See e.g. the various essays in Craig Ott and Harold Netland, eds., *Globalizing Theology: Belief and Practice in an Era of World Christianity* (Grand Rapids: Baker Academic, 2006).

6. Philip Jenkins, *The Next Christendom: The Coming of Global Christianity* (New York: Oxford University Press, 2002), p. 2.

7. Robert L. Browning and Roy A. Reed, *Forgiveness, Reconciliation, and Moral Courage: Motives and Designs for Ministry in a Troubled World* (Grand Rapids: Eerdmans, 2004), p. 50.

8. A recent parable-like news story reported the discovery of an Italian woman who was so terrified by a bout of influenza that she sealed herself in her apartment for twenty-six years to avoid contact with germs. Her brother regularly left tinned food outside the door, and her only communication with neighbors was shouted through the door. When health officials arrived to investigate they were forced to don respirators because of the stench in her apartment. "Italian Recluse Taken from Apartment after 26 Years," retrieved January 28, 2008, from http://www.tiscali.co.uk/news/newswire.php/news/reuters/2006/09/10/odd/italian-recluse-taken-from-apartment-after-26-years.html&template=/news/feeds/story_template.html.

9. As Olthuis puts it, "community, mutuality, neighborliness, intersubjectivity are constitutive of the very nature of each human person . . . in distinction from any form of individualism . . . neighborly love is not a choice. It is an inherent dimension of being human." Conversely, "Disconnection and isolation from God, ourselves, other people and creation is sin and evil. Be(com)ing a whole person is experiencing (re)connection with others (intimacy), realizing my (re)connection with the rest of creation (solidarity), and realizing my root, ground, source, deliverance and healing in the love and grace of God." James H. Olthuis, "Be(com)ing: Humankind as Gift and Call," *Philosophia Reformata* 58 (1993): 153-72, at pp. 160-161, 172.

10. World Tourism Organization, *Tourism Highlights 2007 Edition* (Madrid: UNWTO, 2007).

11. Thomas I. Wortman, "Psychosocial Effects of Studying Abroad: Openness to Diversity," *Dissertation Abstracts International* 63, no. 07A (2002), p. 2479.

12. Giancarlo Collet, "From Theological Vandalism to Theological Romanticism? Questions about a Multicultural Identity of Christianity," in *Christianity and Cultures,* ed. Norbert Greinacher and Norbert Mette (London: SCM; Maryknoll, N.Y.: Orbis, 1994), pp. 25-37.

13. Michael Byram contrasts the tourist, who wants life to be "enriched but not fundamentally changed" through encounter with cultural others, and the sojourner, who enters into more substantial and vulnerable relationships; see Michael Byram, *Teaching and Assessing Intercultural Communicative Competence* (Clevedon: Multilingual Matters, 1997), pp. 1-2.

14. Tzvetan Todorov, *On Human Diversity: Nationalism, Racism, and Exoticism in French Thought* (Cambridge, Mass.: Harvard University Press, 1993), pp. 342, 345.

15. John Durham Peters, *Speaking into the Air: A History of the Idea of Communication* (Chicago: University of Chicago Press, 1999).

16. "Chilondoscow" (Chicago + London + Moscow) is one of the composite places in which AT&T subscribers are promised connectivity in a current series of TV and billboard advertisements. The question about speaking global is from a BT advertisement in *Fortune* magazine (156 no. 10, November 12, 2007, p. 103). The "press here" promise is from an advertisement for Palm® smart phones in *Business Week* magazine (no. 4059, November 19, 2007, pp. 56-57).

17. The case study described in the following paragraphs is from Julie A. Belz, "Linguistic Perspectives on the Development of Intercultural Competence in Telecollaboration," *Language Learning and Technology* 7, no. 2 (2003): 68-89, retrieved from http://llt.msu.edu/vol7num3/belz/, November 13, 2007. See also Julie A. Belz, "Institutional and Individual Dimensions of Transatlantic Group Work in Network-Based Language Teaching," *ReCALL* 13, no. 2 (2001): 213-31; Julie A. Belz, "Social Dimensions of Telecollaborative Language Study," *Language Learning and Technology* 6, no. 1 (2002): 60-81, retrieved from http://llt.msu.edu/vol6num1/belz/, November 13, 2007; Julie A. Belz and Andreas Müller-Hartmann, "Deutsch-amerikanische Telekollaboration im Fremdsprachenunterricht — Lernende im Kreuzfeuer der institutionellen Zwänge," *Die Unterrichtspraxis* 35, no. 1 (2002): 68-78.

18. See Heidi Byrnes, "Interactional Style in German and American Conversations," *Text* 6, no. 2 (1986): 189-206.

19. Belz, "Linguistic Perspectives," p. 78. This email message and those that follow are quoted with their original typographic errors.

20. Belz, "Linguistic Perspectives," p. 80.

21. Belz, "Linguistic Perspectives," p. 83; coding of particular phrases has been removed.

22. As Belz puts it, "In effect, the very medium that is touted as the cost-effective means of bringing sets of 'others' together for the purposes of fostering

intercultural understanding may simultaneously exacerbate the realization of this educational goal." Belz, "Linguistic Perspectives," p. 78.

23. Nicholas Ostler, *Empires of the Word: A Language History of the World* (New York: HarperCollins, 2005), p. 456.

24. David Crystal, *English as a Global Language,* 2d ed. (Cambridge: Cambridge University Press, 2003), p. 9.

25. Molly Wieland, "Turn-Taking Structure as a Source of Misunderstanding in French-American Cross-Cultural Conversation," in *Pragmatics and Language Learning,* vol. 2, ed. Lawrence Bouton and Yamuna Kachru (Urbana: Division of English as an International Language, University of Illinois at Urbana-Champaign, 1991), pp. 101-18.

26. Crystal, *English as a Global Language,* p. 69.

27. Crystal, *English as a Global Language,* pp. 118-19.

28. More precisely, the learning of English will for many have served as the precondition for gaining access to education and prosperity; see Alastair Pennycook, *The Cultural Politics of English as an International Language* (London: Longman, 1994), pp. 14-21.

29. Lesslie Newbigin, *Foolishness to the Greeks: The Gospel and Western Culture* (Grand Rapids: Eerdmans, 1986), p. 22.

30. As Pennycook puts it, "The global position of English means that it is situated in many contexts that are specific to that globalization: to use English implies relationships to local conditions of social and economic prestige, to certain forms of culture and knowledge, and also to global relations of capitalism and particular global discourses of democracy, economics, the environment, popular culture, modernity, development, education and so on. The particular position of English suggests that these relationships, both local and global, will be very different from those between other languages and discourses." Pennycook, *Cultural Politics,* p. 34.

31. Crystal, *English as a Global Language,* p. 78.

32. The reference to renaming as release from insignificance is from James Boyce, "'Robert May': Real Name Forever Lost," *Tasmania, 40° South* 35 (2004): 45-47, at p. 47; the other examples are from Crystal, *English as a Global Language,* pp. 124-25.

33. Crystal, *English as a Global Language,* pp. 124-25.

34. Y. Tsuda, cited in Robert Phillipson and Tove Skutnabb-Kangas, "English Only Worldwide or Language Ecology?" *TESOL Quarterly* 30, no. 3 (1996): 429-52, at p. 430. On the importance of reciprocity in Asian cultural settings, see further the discussion of a British-Chinese business meeting below.

35. There is a motto that surfaces in various discussion boards online as an expression of support for the military: "If you are reading this, thank a teacher. If you are reading this in English, thank a soldier." It does not seem to occur to posters to question why speaking English rather than another language should automatically be viewed as a superior state of affairs, or whether the motto might sug-

gest rather different and more sinister meanings when read by a native speaker of a language other than English, or even that many who read the posts may in fact not be native speakers of English.

36. Phillipson notes that "at the interpersonal level it is highly likely that those operating in English as a foreign language are less convincing than in their own languages." This places the voices of non-English speakers at a disadvantage where English is maintained as the only medium of participation in processes such as academic and diplomatic exchange. Robert Phillipson, "Globalizing English: Are Linguistic Human Rights an Alternative to Linguistic Imperialism?" *Language Sciences* 20, no. 1 (1998): 101-12, at p. 107. On the relevance of this to participation of global Christian leaders and theologians in theological discussion, see also Tite Tiénou, "Christian Theology in an Era of World Christianity," in Ott and Netland, eds., *Globalizing Theology,* pp. 37-51, esp. pp. 48-50.

37. Helen Spencer-Oatey and Jianyu Xing, "Managing Talk and Non-Talk in Intercultural Interactions: Insights from Two Chinese-British Business Meetings," *Multilingua* 24 (2005): 55-74, at pp. 67-68.

38. Spencer-Oatey and Xing, "Managing Talk," p. 69. The quote is translated from Chinese.

39. Brian J. Walsh, "From Housing to Homemaking: Worldviews and the Shaping of Home," *Christian Scholar's Review* 35, no. 2 (2006): 237-57.

40. Walsh, "Housing to Homemaking," p. 239.

41. Walsh, "Housing to Homemaking," p. 240.

42. Walsh, "Housing to Homemaking," p. 241.

43. Paja Lee Donnelly, "Ethics and Cross-Cultural Nursing," *Journal of Transcultural Nursing* 11, no. 2 (2000): 119-26, at p. 123.

44. Donnelly, "Ethics and Cross-Cultural Nursing," p. 123.

45. Richard E. Nisbett, *The Geography of Thought: How Asians and Westerners Think Differently . . . and Why* (New York: The Free Press, 2003), p. 211.

46. Lisa Delpit, *Other People's Children: Cultural Conflict in the Classroom* (New York: The New Press, 1995), p. 22.

47. See Cornelius Plantinga Jr., *Engaging God's World: A Reformed Vision of Faith, Learning, and Living* (Grand Rapids: Eerdmans, 2002), pp. 103-36.

Notes to Chapter 6

1. For a systematic survey of learning objectives involved in gaining the ability to communicate interculturally, see Michael Byram, *Teaching and Assessing Intercultural Communicative Competence* (Clevedon: Multilingual Matters, 1997), pp. 1-2.

2. Dell H. Hymes, *Ethnography, Linguistics, Narrative Inequality: Toward an Understanding of Voice* (London: Taylor and Francis, 1996), pp. 84-85. Hymes's list contains two more entries: "Differences in language are essentially of two kinds,

right and wrong"; and "Verbal fluency and noticeable style are suspicious, except as entertainment (it's what you mean that counts)."

3. Timothy Regan, *Language, Education, and Ideology: Mapping the Linguistic Landscape of U.S. Schools* (Westport, Conn.: Praeger, 2002), p. 16.

4. Umberto Eco, *Serendipities: Language and Lunacy* (London: Phoenix, 1999), p. 71.

5. Eco, *Serendipities*, p. 72.

6. Duane Elmer, *Cross-Cultural Servanthood: Serving the World in Christlike Humility* (Downers Grove, Ill.: InterVarsity Press, 2006), p. 147.

7. Anne Fadiman, *The Spirit Catches You and You Fall Down: A Hmong Child, Her American Doctors, and the Collision of Two Cultures* (New York: Farrar, Straus and Giroux, 1997), p. 112.

8. David I. Smith and Barbara Carvill, *The Gift of the Stranger: Faith, Hospitality, and Foreign Language Learning* (Grand Rapids: Eerdmans, 2000), p. 63.

9. Z. D. Gurevitch, "The Power of Not Understanding: The Meeting of Conflicting Identities," *Journal of Applied Behavioral Sciences* 25, no. 2 (1989): 161-73, at p. 163.

10. Mark R. Schwehn, *Exiles from Eden: Religion and the Academic Vocation in America* (New York: Oxford University Press, 1993), p. 48.

11. Schwehn, *Exiles from Eden*, p. 49.

12. Christine Pohl, *Making Room: Recovering Hospitality as a Christian Tradition* (Grand Rapids: Eerdmans, 1999), p. 69.

13. See Luke Bretherton, *Hospitality as Holiness: Christian Witness amid Moral Diversity* (Aldershot: Ashgate, 2006).

14. Smith and Carvill, *Gift of the Stranger*, pp. 91-92.

15. Schwehn, *Exiles from Eden*, p. 44.

16. Fadiman, *The Spirit Catches You*, p. 95.

17. Smith and Carvill, *Gift of the Stranger*, p. 70. See also Mary Buteyn, "When 'evangelisch' Is not 'Evangelical': Preparing Students for a Different Religious Culture," *Journal of Christianity and Foreign Languages* 8 (2007): 61-66.

18. Mikhail M. Bakhtin, *Speech Genres and Other Late Essays*, trans. Vern W. McGee (Austin: University of Texas Press, 1986), p. 7.

19. Cited in Alan Jacobs, "Bakhtin and the Hermeneutics of Love," in *Bakhtin and Religion: A Feeling for Faith*, ed. Susan M. Felch and Paul J. Contino (Evanston: Northwestern University Press, 2001), pp. 25-45, at p. 27.

20. David I. Smith, "Egocentricity and Learning to Hear a Foreign Language," *Journal of Christianity and Foreign Languages* 8 (2007): 3-8.

21. I am grateful to Hadley Wood for the story and permission to use it.

22. Miroslav Volf, "A Vision of Embrace: Theological Perspectives on Cultural Identity and Conflict," *Ecumenical Review* 48, no. 2 (1995): 195-205, at p. 203.

23. Elmer, *Cross-Cultural Servanthood*, pp. 93-104.

24. Miroslav Volf, *Exclusion and Embrace: A Theological Exploration of Identity, Otherness, and Reconciliation* (Nashville: Abingdon Press, 1996), p. 126.

25. Volf, *Exclusion and Embrace*, p. 127.

26. Volf, *Exclusion and Embrace*, p. 129.

27. Amy G. Oden, ed., *And You Welcomed Me: A Sourcebook on Hospitality in Early Christianity* (Nashville: Abingdon Press, 2001), p. 15.

28. Volf, "A Vision of Embrace," p. 197.

Notes to Chapter 7

1. For the sociological details drawn upon here, see David A. Fiensy, "The Composition of the Jerusalem Church," in *The Book of Acts in Its First-Century Setting*, vol. 4, ed. Richard Bauckham (Grand Rapids: Eerdmans, 1995), pp. 213-36.

2. Ben Witherington III, *The Acts of the Apostles: A Socio-Rhetorical Commentary* (Grand Rapids: Eerdmans, 1998), p. 132. My concern in this chapter is not with the pneumatological implications of Pentecost, but with its implications for how Christians (ought to) think about cultural diversity. This does not, of course, in any way exclude or imply the unimportance of readings of Pentecost that focus on other aspects of the Spirit's work.

3. James D. G. Dunn, *The Acts of the Apostles* (Valley Forge, Pa.: Trinity Press International, 1996), pp. 23-24. Fire was a widespread symbol of Torah in Judaism; see Luke Timothy Johnson, *The Acts of the Apostles*, Sacra Pagina, vol. 5 (Collegeville, Minn.: Liturgical Press, 1992), p. 46. A rabbinic legend taught that when the Law was given, the voice was divided into seventy languages and each nation heard it in its own language; see F. F. Bruce, *Commentary on the Book of Acts* (Grand Rapids: Eerdmans, 1954), p. 59.

4. Johnson, *Acts*, p. 45.

5. Moore argues that the last phrase points to the ethnic as well as the geographic universality of the gospel. Thomas S. Moore, "To the End of the Earth: The Geographical and Ethnic Universalism of Acts 1:8 in Light of Isaianic Influence on Luke," *Journal of the Evangelical Theological Society* 40, no. 3 (1997): 389-99.

6. Dunn, *Acts*, pp. 9-11.

7. See also Judges 3:9-10: "But when they cried out to the LORD, he raised up for them a deliverer, Othniel son of Kenaz, Caleb's younger brother, who saved them. The Spirit of the LORD came on him, so that he became Israel's judge and went to war. The LORD gave Cushan-Rishathaim king of Aram into the hands of Othniel, who overpowered him."

8. Bruce, *Book of Acts*, p. 56.

9. Charles H. Talbert, *Reading Acts: A Literary and Theological Commentary on the Acts of the Apostles* (New York: Crossroad, 1997), p. 42.

10. There are clear, if complex, parallels between Luke's Pentecost narrative and the Babel narrative in Genesis 11; there is, however, little reason to suspect that the Babel story would have leapt to mind as a model *before* the events of the day of Pentecost, since it contains no reference to the empowerment of the Spirit

or to bearing witness. On the complexities of the relationship between Babel and Pentecost see further David I. Smith, "What Hope after Babel? Diversity and Community in Gen. 11:1-9, Exod. 1:1-14, Zeph. 3:1-13 and Acts 2:1-13," *Horizons in Biblical Theology* 18, no. 2 (1996): 169-91.

11. Bruce, *Book of Acts,* p. 54.

12. Witherington notes that Luke is "presenting a Greek summary of a Jewish speech, perhaps even a speech originally in Aramaic spoken with a Galilean accent"; *Acts,* p. 138.

13. This contrasts with the ancient Greek and Roman tendency to classify foreigners as "barbarians," i.e., those who speak incomprehensibly or crudely, a tendency absorbed to some degree by the church in later centuries as it imbibed Greco-Roman learning; see David I. Smith and Barbara Carvill, *The Gift of the Stranger: Faith, Hospitality and Foreign Language Learning* (Grand Rapids: Eerdmans, 2000), pp. 20-24. Interestingly, when the term "barbarian" comes up in Paul's first epistle to the Corinthians, he applies it first to himself: "If then I do not grasp the meaning of what someone is saying, I am a foreigner [barbarian] to the speaker, and the speaker is a foreigner to me" (1 Corinthians 14:11). Perhaps it is no coincidence that this assertion of symmetrical equality between self and other immediately follows the extended meditation on love in 1 Corinthians 13. As some have pointed out, English speakers might take the hint from Pentecost that we should no more expect others to be subject to English than the crowd at Pentecost were made subject to Aramaic. See Ajith Fernando, *Acts,* NIV Application Commentary (Grand Rapids: Zondervan, 1998), p. 96; Justo L. González, "For the Healing of the Nations: The Book of Revelation and Our Multicultural Calling," in *The One in the Many: Christian Identity in a Multicultural World,* ed. Thomas R. Thompson (Lanham, Md.: University Press of America, 1998), p. 1.

14. There is a long (though by no means universal) tradition of reading the Babel narrative in Genesis 11 in terms of a golden age in which all spoke one language followed by God's judgment, resulting in linguistic diversity. On this reading of Babel it becomes difficult to accept a parallel between Babel and Pentecost, since a redeeming of Babel would then need to involve a return to a single language (see, e.g., Dunn, *Acts,* p. 24). There are, however, a range of good reasons for questioning this reading of Babel (and therefore rethinking its relationship to Pentecost), including the association of the "one speech" motif of Genesis 11:1 with imperial conquest in archeological records, the choice of redirection instead of destruction after the promise in Genesis 9 not to send another flood, the assertions of apparently unproblematic linguistic diversity in Genesis 10, and the emphasis at the end of the Babel story that people had been returned to (a chastened version of) what they had been repeatedly commanded to do since the start of Genesis, namely spread out and fill the earth. On a reading that takes these and other details of the text seriously, the "one speech" is not innocent, and the scattering is not all bad. As Walter Brueggemann puts it, Babel "attempts to establish a cultural, human oneness without reference to the threats, promises or mandates

of God. This is a self-made unity in which humanity has a 'fortress mentality.' It seeks to survive by its own resources. It seeks to construct a world free of the danger of the holy and immune from the terrors of God in history. It is a unity grounded in fear and characterized by coercion. A human unity without the vision of God's will is likely to be ordered in oppressive conformity. And it will finally be 'in vain.'" See Walter Brueggemann, *Genesis* (Atlanta: John Knox, 1982), p. 99. For a similar reading, see Frank D. Macchia, "Unity and Otherness: Lessons from Babel and Pentecost," *The Living Pulpit* 13, no. 4 (2004): 5-7. On the interpretive issues in Genesis 11 see further Smith, "What Hope." For the textual evidence that Luke's Pentecost narrative alludes to Genesis 11, see J. G. Davies, "Pentecost and Glossolalia," *Journal of Theological Studies* 3 (1952): 228-31. Various commentators have expressed doubt concerning the connection between Pentecost and Babel, but the usual argument, that Pentecost does not show a return to a single language, becomes irrelevant if Babel is not in fact about a monolingual golden age.

15. *Hymns on Paradise* 11.14, cited in *Acts,* Ancient Christian Commentary on Scripture, New Testament V, ed. Francis Martin (Downers Grove, Ill.: InterVarsity Press, 2006), pp. 20-21.

16. Fiensy, "Composition of the Jerusalem Church," pp. 230-31.

17. Fiensy, "Composition of the Jerusalem Church," pp. 234-35. Fiensy points out that some of these (on both sides of the divide) could have been Jews who came for the festival and stayed in Jerusalem after joining the church, but that it is most likely that most of them (again on both sides) were inhabitants of Jerusalem, reflecting its existing social and cultural constitution.

18. Fiensy, "Composition of the Jerusalem Church," p. 214.

19. Witherington suggests that "[t]he point is not to provide a tour of the known world but to mention nations that had known extensive Jewish populations" (*Acts,* p. 136).

20. "If we follow the majority text, the city of Sebaste must be referred to. The reason for referring to it by an obsolete name was probably to underline its connection with the lost northern kingdom and the lost sheep of the house of Israel." David Seccombe, "The New People of God," in *Witness to the Gospel: The Theology of Acts,* ed. I. Howard Marshall and David Peterson (Grand Rapids: Eerdmans, 1998), p. 359.

21. Seccombe, "New People of God," p. 359.

22. An alternative view argues that the term "eunuch" had at this point in time come to designate royal officials in general, because of the historical preponderance of actual eunuchs in such roles, and might not on this occasion mean a literal eunuch. See, e.g., Bertram L. Melbourne, "Acts 1–8 Re-examined: Is Acts 8 Its Fulfillment?" *Journal of Religious Thought* 57/58, no. 2/1/2 (2005): 1-18. If this view is correct, then the progression in Acts 8 is simply from Samaritans, with their contested Israelite heritage, to entirely foreign converts, although Luke's use of the term "eunuch," even if not literal, may still have evoked marginality in a Jewish context.

23. Terence L. Donaldson, ed., *Religious Rivalries and the Struggle for Success in Caesarea Maritima* (Waterloo, Ont.: Canadian Corporation for Studies in Religion and Wilfrid Laurier University Press, 2000).

24. Wendy Cotter, "Cornelius, the Roman Army, and Religion," in Donaldson, ed., *Religious Rivalries*, p. 283.

25. Some (e.g., Talbert, *Reading Acts*, p. 104) have suggested that the fact that Peter is staying at the house of "Simon the tanner" (Acts 10:6) suggests that he has already concluded that the purity regulations no longer bind him, for tanners were considered unclean because of their handling of carcasses. Miller has recently argued that while tanners were clearly of low social status, they were not necessarily therefore outcasts in terms of religious uncleanness, and that Peter's vigorous defense of the ritual purity of his eating habits when confronted by his vision does not suggest someone who has already turned his back on such regulations. Chris A. Miller, "Did Peter's Vision in Acts 10 Pertain to Men or the Menu?" *Bibliotheca Sacra* 159 (2002): 302-17, at pp. 303-4.

26. Miller, "Peter's Vision." Miller notes that one so sympathetic to the Jews as Cornelius, and so eager to revere Peter, for whose visit he had several days to prepare, would have been highly unlikely to serve non-kosher food to his guest (p. 310).

27. It is interesting to consider the parallels with a much earlier episode of divinely commissioned lunchtime visitors. In Genesis 18 we find Abraham "sitting at the entrance to his tent in the heat of the day," and suddenly he sees "three men standing nearby" (18:1-2). Reflecting the high value placed on hospitality in his culture, Abraham hurries to invite them to stay and eat. As the tale unfolds, something curious happens: the narrative flips back and forth between "they said" and "the Lord said" when reporting the men's speech (18:5, 9, 10, 13, 16, 17, 33). In the form of these three visitors, it is God himself who visits Abraham, and by welcoming strangers Abraham finds that he has given God space to speak a life-altering word to him. The three men deliver the promise that Sarah, however ridiculous the idea might seem, will bear a son (v. 10). "Surely not," is Sarah's incredulous response (18:12), but it is overruled. The promise that "all peoples on earth" will be blessed through Abraham (12:3), and that his descendents will be as numerous as the stars, thus begins to be fulfilled, and Abraham becomes the father of the Israelites. Returning to Luke's account, we find that it is around noon, that lunch is being prepared, that Peter hears a word from God that he is initially unable to accept, that three men show up who turn out to be sent by God, and that Peter invites them in for food (Acts 10:9, 10, 14, 22, 23). This act of hospitality turns out to be the start of the church's realization that the church will indeed be composed of "all peoples on earth." God is redrawing the boundaries of his people and redefining who is a child of Abraham.

28. Gaventa analyzes the structure of the story as comprising eight scenes in which a studied series of symmetries leads to the joining of Jew and Gentile. The scenes are as follows: A. Visions: 1. Cornelius (10:1-8); 2. Peter (9-16); B. Journey

and Welcome: 3. Cornelius (17-23a); 4. Peter (23b-29); C. Speeches: 5. Cornelius (30-33); 6. Peter (34-43); D. Confirmation: 7. Holy Spirit (44-48); 8. Community (11:1-18). Beverly Roberts Gaventa, *The Acts of the Apostles* (Nashville: Abingdon Press, 2003), p. 163. Note the priority of Cornelius in each pair of scenes.

29. Throughout the encounter with Cornelius we are reminded that it is not simply a meeting of individuals, but rather an encounter with the whole of Cornelius's household, from which he is not separated. Issues of hospitality and fellowship are thus to the fore. See Ronald D. Witherup, "Cornelius Over and Over and Over Again: 'Functional Redundancy' in the Acts of the Apostles," *Journal for the Study of the New Testament* 49 (1993): 45-66, at p. 50.

30. Lim Yeu Chuen, "Acts 10: A Gentile Model for Pentecostal Experience," *Asian Journal of Pentecostal Studies* 1, no. 1 (1998): 62-72.

31. The chapter plays frequently on words for house and household and on the crossing of thresholds, subtly underscoring the theme of mixing between groups that previously excluded one another; for detailed discussion see Miller, "Peter's Vision," pp. 311-13.

32. "The verb *katalambanomai* is in the present tense, middle voice, showing action in progress for the benefit of the speaker. A better rendering would be: 'I am just now coming to perceive for myself that God is not partial.' At that very moment Peter was in the process of coming to a personal realization of this truth about God." J. Julius Scott, "The Cornelius Incident in the Light of Its Jewish Setting," *Journal of the Evangelical Theological Society* 34, no. 4 (1991): 475-84, at p. 483.

33. Witherup, "Cornelius Over and Over and Over Again," p. 52.

34. Scott points out that in Acts 10:28, when Peter specifies those with whom Jews are not to associate, "*Allophylos* (which occurs only here in the NT), literally 'of another tribe,' is used rather than *athemitos*, 'foreigner' or 'Gentile.' . . . *Allophylos* is commonly used in the LXX for, among other things, Philistines." Scott suggests that "*allophylos* may be a precise term used in the first century to refer to uncircumcised persons present in the land of Israel, thus similar to the Hebrew *gēr.*" If this suggestion has merit, it underlines the relevance to this episode of earlier admonitions to "love the stranger *(gēr).*" Scott, "Cornelius Incident," p. 479.

35. Cf. Benny Tat-siong Liew, "Acts," in *Global Bible Commentary,* ed. Daniel Patte (Nashville: Abingdon Press, 2004), pp. 419-28.

36. Seccombe, "New People," p. 350.

37. Andrew Walls, *The Cross-Cultural Process in Christian History* (Maryknoll, N.Y.: Orbis, 2002), p. 13.

38. Walls, *Cross-Cultural Process,* p. 29.

39. Walls, *Cross-Cultural Process,* p. 31.

40. Sanneh comments: "If you remember, I said earlier that conversion was to God; I did not say that it was to European or other people's theories of God. I accept that conversion puts the gospel through the crucible of its host culture, but

Europe is not host to Africa in the things of God, do you think?" Lamin Sanneh, *Whose Religion Is Christianity? The Gospel Beyond the West* (Grand Rapids: Eerdmans, 2003), p. 53.

41. Philip Jenkins, *The Next Christendom: The Coming of Global Christianity* (New York: Oxford University Press, 2002), p. 90.

42. See, e.g., Paul-Gordon Chandler, *God's Global Mosaic: What We Can Learn from Christians Around the World* (Downers Grove, Ill.: InterVarsity Press, 2000).

43. Walls, *Cross-Cultural Process*, p. 79, alluding to Ephesians 4:13.

44. Walls suggests that the "question at the Ephesian moment is whether or not the church in all its diversity will demonstrate its unity by the interactive participation of all its culture-specific segments, the interactive participation that is to be expected in a functioning body." Walls, *Cross-Cultural Process*, p. 81.

45. González, "For the Healing of the Nations."

Notes to the Epilogue

1. François Mauriac, *Vipers' Tangle,* trans. Warre B. Wells (Garden City, N.Y.: Image Books, 1957), p. 151.

2. Mauriac, *Vipers' Tangle,* p. 172.

3. Mauriac, *Vipers' Tangle,* p. 177.

Bibliography

Altmann, Gerry T. M. *The Ascent of Babel: An Exploration of Language, Mind and Understanding.* New York: Oxford University Press, 1997.

Ash, Anthony Lee. *The Gospel According to Luke Part II: 9:51–24:53.* Austin: Sweet Publishing Company, 1973.

Augustine. *Confessions.* Translated by Henry Chadwick. New York: Oxford University Press, 1991.

Axtell, Roger E. *Gestures: The Do's and Taboos of Body Language Around the World.* Revised edition. New York: John Wiley & Sons, 1998.

Bailey, Kenneth E. *Poet and Peasant and Through Peasant Eyes: A Literary-Cultural Approach to the Parables in Luke.* Grand Rapids: Eerdmans, 1983.

Bakhtin, Mikhail M. *Speech Genres and Other Late Essays.* Translated by Vern W. McGee. Austin: University of Texas Press, 1986.

Bartholomew, Craig G., and Michael W. Goheen. *The Drama of Scripture: Finding Our Place in the Biblical Story.* Grand Rapids: Baker Academic, 2004.

Bauckham, Richard. "The Scrupulous Priest and the Good Samaritan: Jesus' Parabolic Interpretation of the Law of Moses." *New Testament Studies* 44 (1998): 475-89.

Belz, Julie A. "Institutional and Individual Dimensions of Transatlantic Group Work in Network-Based Language Teaching." *ReCALL* 13, no. 2 (2001): 213-31.

———. "Social Dimensions of Telecollaborative Language Study." *Language Learning and Technology* 6, no. 1 (2002): 60-81. Retrieved from http://llt.msu.edu/vol6num1/belz/, November 13, 2007.

———. "Linguistic Perspectives on the Development of Intercultural Competence in Telecollaboration." *Language Learning and Technology* 7, no. 2

(2003): 68-89. Retrieved from http://llt.msu.edu/vol7num3/belz/, November 13, 2007.

Belz, Julie A., and Andreas Müller-Hartmann. "Deutsch-amerikanische Telekollaboration im Fremdsprachenunterricht — Lernende im Kreuzfeuer der institutionellen Zwänge." *Die Unterrichtspraxis* 35, no. 1 (2002): 68-78.

Bock, Darrell L. *Luke, Volume 2: 9:51–24:53.* Baker Exegetical Commentary on the New Testament. Grand Rapids: Baker Books, 1996.

Borgman, Paul. *Genesis: The Story We Haven't Heard.* Downers Grove, Ill.: InterVarsity Press, 2001.

Boyce, James. "'Robert May': Real Name Forever Lost." *Tasmania, 40° South* 35 (2004): 45-47.

Branch, Robin Gallagher. "Genesis 20: A Literary Template for the Prophetic Tradition." *In die Skriftig* 38, no. 2 (2004): 217-34.

Bretherton, Luke. *Hospitality as Holiness: Christian Witness amid Moral Diversity.* Aldershot: Ashgate, 2006.

Browning, Robert L., and Roy A. Reed. *Forgiveness, Reconciliation, and Moral Courage: Motives and Designs for Ministry in a Troubled World.* Grand Rapids: Eerdmans, 2004.

Bruce, F. F. *Commentary on the Book of Acts.* Grand Rapids: Eerdmans, 1954.

Brueggemann, Walter. *Genesis.* Atlanta: John Knox, 1982.

Búason, Kristján. "The Good Samaritan, Luke 10:25-37: One Text, Three Methods." In *Luke-Acts: Scandinavian Perspectives,* edited by Petri Luomanen. Helsinki: The Finnish Exegetical Society; Göttingen: Vandenhoek & Ruprecht, 1991.

Buteyn, Mary. "When 'evangelisch' Is Not 'Evangelical': Preparing Students for a Different Religious Culture." *Journal of Christianity and Foreign Languages* 8 (2007): 61-66.

Byram, Michael. *Teaching and Assessing Intercultural Communicative Competence.* Clevedon: Multilingual Matters, 1997.

Byrnes, Heidi. "Interactional Style in German and American Conversations." *Text* 6, no. 2 (1986): 189-206.

Calvin, John. *Institutes of the Christian Religion.* Edited by John T. McNeill, translated by Ford Lewis Battles. Philadelphia: Westminster Press, 1960.

Cassuto, Umberto. *A Commentary on the Book of Genesis,* volume 2. Translated by J. Abrahams. Jerusalem: Magnes Press, 1964.

Chandler, Paul-Gordon. *God's Global Mosaic: What We Can Learn from Christians around the World.* Downers Grove, Ill.: InterVarsity Press, 2000.

Chuen, Lim Yeu. "Acts 10: A Gentile Model for Pentecostal Experience." *Asian Journal of Pentecostal Studies* 1, no. 1 (1998): 62-72.

Collet, Giancarlo. "From Theological Vandalism to Theological Romanticism? Questions about a Multicultural Identity of Christianity." In *Christianity and Cultures,* edited by Norbert Greinacher and Norbert Mette. Maryknoll, N.Y.: Orbis Books, 1994.

Cotter, Wendy. "Cornelius, the Roman Army, and Religion." In *Religious Rivalries and the Struggle for Success in Caesarea Maritima,* edited by Terence L. Donaldson. Waterloo, Ont.: Canadian Corporation for Studies in Religion and Wilfrid Laurier University Press, 2000.

Crystal, David. *English as a Global Language.* Second edition. Cambridge: Cambridge University Press, 2003.

Davies, J. G. "Pentecost and Glossolalia." *Journal of Theological Studies,* n.s., 3 (1952): 228-31.

De La Torre, Miguel A. *Reading the Bible from the Margins.* Maryknoll, N.Y.: Orbis Books, 2003.

Delpit, Lisa. *Other People's Children: Cultural Conflict in the Classroom.* New York: The New Press, 1995.

Dillard, Raymond B. *2 Chronicles.* Word Biblical Commentary. Waco: Word Books, 1987.

Donaldson, Terence L., ed. *Religious Rivalries and the Struggle for Success in Caesarea Maritima.* Waterloo, Ont.: Canadian Corporation for Studies in Religion and Wilfrid Laurier University Press, 2000.

Donnelly, Paja Lee. "Ethics and Cross-Cultural Nursing." *Journal of Transcultural Nursing* 11, no. 2 (2000): 119-26.

Dunn, James D. G. *The Acts of the Apostles.* Valley Forge, Pa.: Trinity Press International, 1996.

Eco, Umberto. *Serendipities: Language and Lunacy.* London: Phoenix, 1999.

Ellul, Jacques. *The Humiliation of the Word.* Grand Rapids: Eerdmans, 1985.

Elmer, Duane. *Cross-Cultural Servanthood: Serving the World in Christlike Humility.* Downers Grove, Ill.: InterVarsity Press, 2006.

Enns, Peter. *Inspiration and Incarnation: Evangelicals and the Problem of the Old Testament.* Grand Rapids: Baker Academic, 2005.

Esler, Philip F. "Jesus and the Reduction of Intergroup Conflict: The Parable of the Good Samaritan in the Light of Social Identity Theory." *Biblical Interpretation* 8, no. 4 (2000): 325-57.

Fadiman, Anne. *The Spirit Catches You and You Fall Down: A Hmong Child, Her American Doctors, and the Collision of Two Cultures.* New York: Farrar, Straus and Giroux, 1997.

Fernando, Ajith. *Acts.* NIV Application Commentary. Grand Rapids: Zondervan, 1998.

Fiensy, David A. "The Composition of the Jerusalem Church." In *The Book of Acts in Its First-Century Setting,* volume 4, edited by Richard Bauckham. Grand Rapids: Eerdmans, 1995.

Fox, Kate. *Watching the English: The Hidden Rules of English Behavior.* London: Hodder & Stoughton, 2004.

Freire, Paulo. *Pedagogy of the Oppressed.* New York: Continuum, 2000.

Funk, Robert W. "The Good Samaritan as Metaphor." *Semeia* 2 (1974): 75-84.

Gaventa, Beverly Roberts. *The Acts of the Apostles.* Nashville: Abingdon Press, 2003.

Gnanavaram, M. "'Dalit Theology' and the Parable of the Good Samaritan." *Journal for the Study of the New Testament* 50 (1993): 59-83.

González, Justo L. "For the Healing of the Nations: The Book of Revelation and Our Multicultural Calling." In *The One in the Many: Christian Identity in a Multicultural World,* edited by Thomas R. Thompson. Lanham, Md.: University Press of America, 1998.

Gourgues, Michel. "The Priest, the Levite, and the Samaritan Revisited: A Critical Note on Luke 10:31-35." *Journal of Biblical Literature* 117, no. 4 (1998): 709-13.

Gurevitch, Z. D. "The Power of Not Understanding: The Meeting of Conflicting Identities." *Journal of Applied Behavioral Sciences* 25, no. 2 (1989): 161-73.

Hamilton, Victor P. *The Book of Genesis Chapters 18-50.* New International Commentary on the Old Testament. Grand Rapids: Eerdmans, 1995.

Hawn, C. Michael. *Gather into One: Praying and Singing Globally.* Grand Rapids: Eerdmans, 2003.

Heath, Dwight B. "Cultural Variations among Drinking Patterns." In *Drinking Patterns and Their Consequences,* edited by Marcus Grant and Jorge Litvak. Washington: Taylor & Francis, 1998.

Hendrickx, Herman. *The Third Gospel for the Third World, Volume Three — A Travel Narrative I (Luke 9:51–13:21).* Quezon City, Philippines: Claretian Publications, 2000.

Hodges, Bert H. "Perception Is Relative and Veridical: Biblical and Ecological Perspectives on Knowing and Doing the Truth." In *The Reality of Christian Learning,* edited by Harold Heie and David L. Wolfe. Grand Rapids: Eerdmans, 1987.

Hughes, Dewi. *Castrating Culture: A Christian Perspective on Ethnic Identity from the Margins.* Carlisle: Paternoster, 2000.

Hymes, Dell H. *Ethnography, Linguistics, Narrative Inequality: Toward an Understanding of Voice.* London: Taylor and Francis, 1996.

Isaak, Paul John. "Luke." In *Africa Bible Commentary,* edited by Tokunboh Adeyemo. Nairobi, Kenya: WordAlive Publishers; Grand Rapids: Zondervan, 2006.

Jacobs, Alan. "Bakhtin and the Hermeneutics of Love." In *Bakhtin and Reli-*

gion: A Feeling for Faith, edited by Susan M. Felch and Paul J. Contino. Evanston: Northwestern University Press, 2001.

Janzen, J. Gerald. *Genesis 12–50: Abraham and All the Families of the Earth.* International Theological Commentary. Grand Rapids: Eerdmans, 1993.

Jenkins, Philip. *The Next Christendom: The Coming of Global Christianity.* New York: Oxford University Press, 2002.

———. *The New Faces of Christianity: Believing the Bible in the Global South.* New York: Oxford University Press, 2006.

Jeremias, J. Σαμάρεια, Σαμαρίης, Σαμαρίτις. In *Theological Dictionary of the New Testament,* volume 7, edited by Gerhard Friedrich, translated by Geoffrey W. Bromiley. Grand Rapids: Eerdmans, 1971.

Johnson, Luke Timothy. *The Gospel of Luke.* Sacra Pagina Series, volume 3. Collegeville, Minn.: Liturgical Press, 1991.

———. *The Acts of the Apostles.* Sacra Pagina Series, volume 5. Collegeville, Minn.: Liturgical Press, 1992.

Kessler, Martin, and Karel Deurloo. *A Commentary on Genesis: The Book of Beginnings.* Mahwah, N.J.: Paulist Press, 2004.

Kirk, Alan. "'Love Your Enemies': The Golden Rule and Ancient Reciprocity (Luke 6:27-35)." *Journal of Biblical Literature* 122, no. 4 (2003): 667-86.

Kirkman, Rick, and Jeremy Scott. "Baby Blues." *Grand Rapids Press,* September 20, 2007, p. B11.

Knowles, Michael P. "What Was the Victim Wearing? Literary, Economic and Social Contexts for the Parable of the Good Samaritan." *Biblical Interpretation* 12, no. 2 (2004): 145-74.

Liew, Benny Tat-siong. "Acts." In *Global Bible Commentary,* edited by Daniel Patte. Nashville: Abingdon Press, 2004.

Lingenfelter, Sherwood G., and Marvin K. Mayers. *Ministering Cross-culturally: An Incarnational Model for Personal Relationships.* Second edition. Grand Rapids: Baker Academic, 2003.

MacAndrew, Craig, and Robert B. Edgerton. *Drunken Comportment: A Social Explanation.* Chicago: Aldine, 1969.

Macchia, Frank D. "Unity and Otherness: Lessons from Babel and Pentecost." *The Living Pulpit* 13, no. 4 (2004): 5-7.

McFarland, Ian A. "Who Is My Neighbor? The Good Samaritan as a Source for Theological Anthropology." *Modern Theology* 17, no. 1 (2001): 57-66.

Marsh, Charles. *The Beloved Community: How Faith Shapes Social Justice from the Civil Rights Movement to Today.* New York: Basic Books, 2005.

Marshall, Paul. "Living with Our Differences: Values and Beliefs in a Pluralist Society." Paper presented at the EurECA Conference, St. Chrischona, Switzerland, May 9, 1994.

Martin, Francis, ed. *Acts*. Ancient Christian Commentary on Scripture, New Testament V. Downers Grove, Ill.: InterVarsity Press, 2006.

Mathewes, Charles T. "Book One: The Presumptuousness of Autobiography and the Paradoxes of Beginning." In *A Reader's Companion to Augustine's Confessions*, edited by Kim Paffenroth and Robert P. Kennedy. Louisville: Westminster John Knox Press, 2003.

Matthews, Kenneth A. *Genesis 11:27–50:26*. New American Commentary, volume 1B. Nashville: Broadman & Holman, 2005.

Mauriac, François. *Vipers' Tangle*. Translated by Warre B. Wells. Garden City: Image Books, 1957.

Melbourne, Bertram L. "Acts 1–8 Re-examined: Is Acts 8 Its Fulfillment?" *Journal of Religious Thought* 57/58, no. 2/1/2 (2005): 1-18.

Middleton, J. Richard. *The Liberating Image: The Imago Dei in Genesis 1*. Grand Rapids: Brazos, 2005.

Míguez, Néstor O. "La Parábola del Bueno Samaritano. Contexto, Sujeto e Interpretación." *Cuadernos de Teologia* 22 (2003): 65-78.

Miller, Chris A. "Did Peter's Vision in Acts 10 Pertain to Men or the Menu?" *Bibliotheca Sacra* 159 (2002): 302-17.

Moessner, Jeanne Stevenson. "Preaching the Good Samaritan: A Feminist Perspective." *Journal for Preachers* 9, no. 1 (1995): 21-25.

Moore, Thomas S. "To the End of the Earth: The Geographical and Ethnic Universalism of Acts 1:8 in Light of Isaianic Influence on Luke." *Journal of the Evangelical Theological Society* 40, no. 3 (1997): 389-99.

Mouw, Richard J. *He Shines in All That's Fair: Culture and Common Grace*. Grand Rapids: Eerdmans, 2001.

Newton, Michael. *Savage Girls and Wild Boys: A History of Feral Children*. New York: Thomas Dunne Books, 2003.

Newbigin, Lesslie. *Foolishness to the Greeks: The Gospel and Western Culture*. Grand Rapids: Eerdmans, 1986.

Nisbett, Richard E. *The Geography of Thought: How Asians and Westerners Think Differently . . . and Why*. New York: The Free Press, 2003.

Nolland, John. *Luke 9:21–18:34*. Word Biblical Commentary, volume 35B. Dallas: Word Books, 1993.

————. "The Role of Money and Possessions in the Parable of the Prodigal Son (Luke 15:11-32): A Test Case." In *Reading Luke: Interpretation, Reflection, Formation*, edited by Craig G. Bartholomew, Joel B. Green, and Anthony C. Thiselton. Grand Rapids: Zondervan, 2005.

Oden, Amy G., ed. *And You Welcomed Me: A Sourcebook on Hospitality in Early Christianity*. Nashville: Abingdon Press, 2001.

Olson, Bruce. *Bruchko*. Chichester: New Wine Press, 1978.

Olthuis, James H. "Be(com)ing: Humankind as Gift and Call." *Philosophia Reformata* 58 (1993): 153-72.

Ostler, Nicholas. *Empires of the Word: A Language History of the World.* New York: HarperCollins, 2005.

Ott, Craig, and Harold Netland, eds. *Globalizing Theology: Belief and Practice in an Era of World Christianity.* Grand Rapids: Baker Academic, 2006.

Pennycook, Alastair. *The Cultural Politics of English as an International Language.* London: Longman, 1994.

Peters, John Durham. *Speaking into the Air: A History of the Idea of Communication.* Chicago: University of Chicago Press, 1999.

Phillipson, Robert. "Globalizing English: Are Linguistic Human Rights an Alternative to Linguistic Imperialism?" *Language Sciences* 20, no. 1 (1998): 101-12.

Phillipson, Robert, and Tove Skutnabb-Kangas. "English Only Worldwide or Language Ecology?" *TESOL Quarterly* 30, no. 3 (1996): 429-52.

Plantinga, Cornelius Jr. *Engaging God's World: A Reformed Vision of Faith, Learning, and Living.* Grand Rapids: Eerdmans, 2002.

Pohl, Christine. *Making Room: Recovering Hospitality as a Christian Tradition.* Grand Rapids: Eerdmans, 1999.

Regan, Timothy. *Language, Education, and Ideology: Mapping the Linguistic Landscape of U.S. Schools.* Westport, Conn.: Praeger, 2002.

Ritchhart, Ron. *Intellectual Character: What It Is, Why It Matters, and How to Get It.* San Francisco: Jossey Bass, 2004.

Sacks, Robert D. *A Commentary on the Book of Genesis.* Ancient Near Eastern Texts and Studies, volume 6. Lewiston, N.Y.: Edwin Mellen Press, 1990.

Sanneh, Lamin. *Whose Religion Is Christianity? The Gospel Beyond the West.* Grand Rapids: Eerdmans, 2003.

Sarna, Nahum M. *Genesis.* The JPS Torah Commentary. Philadelphia: The Jewish Publication Society, 1989.

Saville-Troike, Muriel. "Cultural Maintenance and 'Vanishing' Languages." In *Text and Context: Cross-Disciplinary Perspectives on Language Study,* edited by Claire Kramsch and Sally McConnell-Ginet. Lexington, Mass.: D. C. Heath & Co., 1992.

Schwehn, Mark R. *Exiles from Eden: Religion and the Academic Vocation in America.* New York: Oxford University Press, 1993.

Scott, J. Julius. "The Cornelius Incident in the Light of Its Jewish Setting." *Journal of the Evangelical Theological Society* 34, no. 4 (1991): 475-84.

Scott, Lindy. "North American Christians and the Latin American Church: Lessons from South of the Border." *Journal of Christianity and Foreign Languages* 3 (2002): 48-75.

Seccombe, David. "The New People of God." In *Witness to the Gospel: The*

Theology of Acts, edited by I. Howard Marshall and David Peterson. Grand Rapids: Eerdmans, 1998.

Smith, David I. "What Hope after Babel? Diversity and Community in Gen. 11:1-9, Exod. 1:1-14, Zeph. 3:1-13 and Acts 2:1-13." *Horizons in Biblical Theology* 18, no. 2 (1996): 169-91.

————. "How Not to Bless the Nations." *Perspectives* (December 2005): 6-11.

————. "Egocentricity and Learning to Hear a Foreign Language." *Journal of Christianity and Foreign Languages* 8 (2007): 3-8.

Smith, David I., and Barbara Carvill. *The Gift of the Stranger: Faith, Hospitality, and Foreign Language Learning.* Grand Rapids: Eerdmans, 2000.

Smith, James K. A. *The Fall of Interpretation: Philosophical Foundations for a Creational Hermeneutic.* Downers Grove, Ill.: InterVarsity Press, 2000.

Spencer-Oatey, Helen, and Jianyu Xing. "Managing Talk and Non-Talk in Intercultural Interactions: Insights from Two Chinese-British Business Meetings." *Multilingua* 24 (2005): 55-74.

Stanglin, Keith D. "The Historical Connection Between the Golden Rule and the Second Greatest Love Commandment." *Journal of Religious Ethics* 33, no. 2 (2005): 357-71.

Talbert, Charles H. *Reading Luke: A Literary and Theological Commentary on the Third Gospel.* New York: Crossroad, 1982.

————. *Reading Acts: A Literary and Theological Commentary on the Acts of the Apostles.* New York: Crossroad, 1997.

Tiénou, Tite. "Christian Theology in an Era of World Christianity." In *Globalizing Theology: Belief and Practice in an Era of World Christianity,* edited by Craig Ott and Harold Netland. Grand Rapids: Baker Academic, 2006.

Todorov, Tzvetan. *On Human Diversity: Nationalism, Racism, and Exoticism in French Thought.* Cambridge, Mass.: Harvard University Press, 1993.

Topel, John. "The Tarnished Golden Rule (Luke 6:31): The Inescapable Radicalness of Christian Ethics." *Theological Studies* 59, no. 3 (Spring 1998): 475-85.

Vande Kopple, William J. "Toward a Christian View of Language." In *Contemporary Literary Theory: A Christian Appraisal,* edited by Clarence Walhout and Leland Ryken. Grand Rapids: Eerdmans, 1991.

Volf, Miroslav. "A Vision of Embrace: Theological Perspectives on Cultural Identity and Conflict." *Ecumenical Review* 48, no. 2 (1995): 195-205.

————. *Exclusion and Embrace: A Theological Exploration of Identity, Otherness, and Reconciliation.* Nashville: Abingdon Press, 1996.

von Rad, Gerhard. *Genesis: A Commentary.* Translated by John H. Marks. London: SCM Press, 1961.

Walls, Andrew F. *The Cross-Cultural Process in Christian History.* Maryknoll, N.Y.: Orbis Books, 2002.

————. "Eusebius Tries Again: The Task of Reconceiving and Re-visioning the Study of Christian History." In *Enlarging the Story: Perspectives on Writing World Christian History,* edited by Wilbert R. Shenk. Maryknoll, N.Y.: Orbis Books, 2002.

Walsh, Brian J. "From Housing to Homemaking: Worldviews and the Shaping of Home." *Christian Scholar's Review* 35, no. 2 (2006): 237-57.

Weinfeld, Moshe. "Sara and Abimelech (Genesis 20) Against the Background of an Assyrian Law and the Genesis Apocryphon." In *Mélanges Bibliques et Orientaux en L'Honneur de M. Matthias Delcor,* edited by A. Caquot, S. Légasse, and M. Tardieu. Kevelaer: Butzon und Bercker, 1985.

Westermann, Claus. *Genesis: A Practical Commentary.* Translated by David E. Green. Grand Rapids: Eerdmans, 1987.

Wieland, Molly. "Turn-Taking Structure as a Source of Misunderstanding in French-American Cross-Cultural Conversation." In *Pragmatics and Language Learning,* volume 2, edited by Lawrence Bouton and Yamuna Kachru. Urbana, Ill.: Division of English as an International Language, University of Illinois at Urbana-Champaign, 1991.

Willis, John T. *Genesis.* Austin: Sweet, 1979.

Witherington, Ben, III. *The Acts of the Apostles: A Socio-Rhetorical Commentary.* Grand Rapids: Eerdmans, 1998.

Witherup, Ronald D. "Cornelius Over and Over and Over Again: 'Functional Redundancy' in the Acts of the Apostles." *Journal for the Study of the New Testament* 49 (1993): 45-66.

World Tourism Organization. *Tourism Highlights 2007 Edition.* Madrid: UNWTO, 2007.

Wortman, Thomas I. "Psychosocial Effects of Studying Abroad: Openness to Diversity." *Dissertation Abstracts International* 63, no. 07A (2002): 2479.

Wright, N. T. *Colossians and Philemon.* Tyndale New Testament Commentaries. Leicester: InterVarsity Press, 1986.

————. *Jesus and the Victory of God.* London: SPCK, 1996.

Index